THE NEW
WAGNERIAN

ALSO BY IAN DALLAS:

The Book of Strangers
The Ten Symphonies of Gorka König
The Time of the Bedouin
Three Plays - 'The Face of Love',
'Statue of David' and 'Oedipus and Dionysus'
Collected Works (plays and prose)
Political Renewal
The Interim is Mine
The Engines of the Broken World

IAN DALLAS

THE NEW WAGNERIAN

BUDGATE PRESS

First edition: Freiburg Books 1991
Second edition: Kutubia Mayurqa 2001
This edition 2013
All rights reserved
budgate@gmail.com

Budgate Press
Postnet Suite 402
Constantia 7848
Cape Town
Republic of South Africa

Subject: Music, Politics, Philosophy

ISBN: 978-0-620-467551-1
Printed by Lightning Source

CONTENTS

"Since the day I heard your music I keep
saying to myself, especially in bad moments:
IF I COULD AT LEAST HEAR
SOME WAGNER THIS EVENING.
Without doubt there are other men like me."

CHARLES BAUDELAIRE

Stammtafel **Spörl** (Saalburg)

Spörel, wohl zu Saalburg (südl. Schlei[z]
* um 1500

Caspar **Spörel,** Bürgermeister zu Saalburg
* um 1530 † vor 1602
∞ um 1550 mit Anna ? * 1530 begr. 5. 5. 1614

Benedictus Spörel, Ratskämmerer zu Saalburg
* um 1550 † vor 1602
∞ um 1575 mit Dorothea ? * 1551 † 1612

Jobst **Spörel,** Bürgermeister zu Saalburg
* 1555 begr. 3. 10. 1619
∞ um 1580 mit Elisabeth ? † 1633 a. d. Pest

Jobst Spörel sen., Braumeister
† nach 1634 ∞ mit ?

Nicol. Spörel jun., (wohl Metzger)
1618 noch ledig † vor 1628
∞ ?

Caspar **Spörel** sen., Bürgermeist[er]
u. Metzger * 1596 begr. 19. 3. 167[x]
∞ mit Barbara ? * 1590 begr. 10. 9. 16[xx]

Jobst Spörel jun.
Brauer * 1612
∞ 5. 5. 1634 mit
Cath. Seuffert aus
Helmsgrün

Maria
* 1622
† 1627

Regina
* 1624
† 1624

Andreas
Metzger
* 1624
† ?
∞ 1648 mit
Barbara Bauer

Nikol
Metzger
* 1625
∞ 1656 mit
Susanna
Schmidt

Susanna
* 1628

Caspar **Spörel** jun.
Bürgermeister u. Metzger
get. 19. 5. 1636 † 3. 4. 1710
∞ 8. 1. 1661 mit
Maria **Göll,** Tochter des
Bürgermeisters Joh. Göll
in Tanna

Rosina **Spörl**
get. 17. 10. 1661
∞ 24. 10. 1682 Großhettstedt
Joh. Georg **Hoë,** Pfarrer zu Großhettstedt

....

Hans Heinr. Spörl
Metzger
get. 5. 5. 1671
∞ 16. 11. 1697
Anna Maria Zimmermann

Joh. Christoph **Hoë**
Bürgermeister, Kauf- und Handelsherr in Stadtilm
get. 10. 6. 1695 Großhettstedt begr. 24. 9. 1755 Stadtilm
∞ 7. 2. 1718 Barbara Maria **Henkel**
get. 13. 8. 1702 Stadtilm † 7. 9. 1776 Stadtilm

Kath. Dorothea **Hoë**
* 13. 1. 1722 † 17. 8. 1784
∞ 15. 11. 1744 Joh. Abrah. **Moßdorf,** Kauf- und Handelsherr
* 26. 10. 1720 † 10. 11. 1768

Johanne Christiane **Moßdorf**
* 15. 3. 1755
∞ 3. 2. 1771 Heinr. Aug. **Pfeifer,** Kurfürstl. Kammersekr. und
Kammerkommiss.
* 5. 5. 1738

Dorothea Juliane Karol. **Pfeifer**
* 4. 1. 1772 † 1835
∞ 10. 4. 1792 Joh. Christ. Friedr. **Hahn,** sächs. Finanzkommiss.
Erbherr auf Wählitz
* Nov. 1761 † 21. 7. 1831

Johanna Elisab. Wilhelmine **Hahn**
* 14. 10. 1794 † 3. 11. 1876
∞ 12. 2. 1816 Dav. Ernst **Oehler,** Pfarrer in Pobles
* 2. 8. 1787 † 17. 12. 1859

Franziska Ernestine Rosaura **Oehler**
* 2. 2. 1826 † 20. 4. 1897
∞ 10. 10. 1843 Karl Ludw. **Nietzsche,** Pfarrer in Röcken
* 10. 10. 1813 † 30. 7. 1849

Friedrich Nietzsche
* 15. 10. 1844 Röcken
† 25. 8. 1900 Weimar

Gemeinsame Vorfahren hatten
Friedrich Nietzsche und Richard
Wagner, wie diese Stammtafel
belegt.

„Der alte" Jobst Spörel zu Saalburg
* um 1530 † vor 1602
∞ um 1550 mit Margarete ? * 1530 begr. 24. 11. 1613

Nicol. **Spörel,** Ratsverwandter zu Saalburg
* 1560? begr. 8. 3. 1610
∞ mit Catharina ? * 1561 begr. 26. 2. 1617

Maria **Spörel,** * um 1600
begr. 16. 11. 1634 Gera
∞ 16. 11. 1619 Gera mit
Barthol **Negler**
Weißgerber in Gera
begr. 25. 10. 1677 Gera

Hans **Nägler**
Weißgerber in Gera
get. 20. 12. 1624 Gera begr. 24. 7. 1664 Gera
∞ 9. 1. 1649 Gera Elisab. **Meyer**
get. 9. 7. 1624 Gera † ?

Jeremias **Nägler**
Weißgerber in Weißenfels
get. 17. 12. 1650 Gera † ?
∞ mit ?

Joh. Wilh. **Nägler**
Weißgerber in Weißenfels
* 11. 9. 1680 Weißenfels † ?
∞ 5. 6. 1703 Maria Rosina **Schnetter**
* 20. 2. 1686 Weißenfels † ?

Maria Rosina **Nägler**
* 7. 8. 1715 Weißenfels † ?
∞ 18. 6. 1737 Joh. Gottfr. **Iglisch,** Bürger u.
Lohgerbermeister in Weißenfels
* 9. 1. 1712 Weißenfels † ?

Dorothea Erdmuthe **Iglisch**
* 30. 6. 1742 Weißenfels † 5. 1. 1789 Weißenfels
∞ 11. 1. 1763 Joh. Gottlob **Pätz,** Bürger u. Weißbäckermeister
in Weißenfels
* 13. 10. 1741 Weißenfels † 17. 1. 1802 Weißenfels

Johanna Rosina **Pätz**
* 19. 11. 1774 Weißenfels † 9. 1. 1848 Leipzig
als verwitw. Geyer
∞ 2. 6. 1798 Friedr. Wilh. **Wagner**
Polizeiaktuar in Leipzig
* 18. 6. 1770 † 23. 11. 1813

Richard Wagner
* 22. 5. 1813 Leipzig
† 13. 2. 1883 Venedig

1

THE MAN AND HIS TIME

Richard Wagner. In the end, if you have entered into the universe of his music dramas you will also have the conviction of having in some way met its creator and that he is your close friend. Do not be put off by the bitterly sarcastic critics, or perhaps, yes, do be put off. If you view life as they do, and envy vastness of spirit and profundity of meditative reflection on existence and nature, and surrender to the erotic drive, yes, do turn away. Wagner is not for you. Idolatry is one of the terms of these critics. It is ironic to note that one of his most bitter critics has gained his immortality simply by having disliked him so much. My first encounter with Wagner was when I was nineteen. And as Schiller counselled, the convictions of one's youth are true and endure, so guard them! I met him through my other passion, Baudelaire. I read in the letter he wrote to the composer after experiencing Tannhäuser, 'Vous m'avez rappelez à moi-même et au grand dans des mauvaises heures.' I went from Tristan to Parsifal, intoxicated by the former, sobered beyond my years by the latter.

Immediate exposure to the 'sound' of Wagner, and we will examine this in detail later, has its immediate and inescapable result. There cannot be indifference – there is recognition or there is not. The ideas of Wagner, or the 'idea' of Wagner in the Heideggerian sense, need a closer study. It is in this context that we must recall that while Wagner achieved a tremendous fame and world reputation – in a sense he was the first modern world master renowned everywhere – he was also way ahead of his time. It is not just that modern music began with the tonalities and chromatic texture of the last Wagner works or that with his profound sense of the future he could declare in 1882 'Music is finished!' – as Heidegger was to declare the end of philosophy less than a century later – it is that there never has been a serious attempt to come to terms with the insights, convictions, and visions which he entertained. Critics have been so dedicatedly attacking his ego, his reputation, and his 'right' to be so lauded, that in the end people were persuaded that there was no need to go deeply into what his ideas were for the future at a political level or what he understood at the intimate level. Of course, his prose writings are notoriously difficult to read. There is an excuse. Yet Nietzsche is renowned for the ease with which he can be read in his glowing and superbly wrought prose, and only now are people beginning to come to terms with the structural patterns of thought beneath the dazzling aphoristic surface. Nietzsche was a philosopher and so in the end there is a textual confrontation that cannot be avoided however much our century has shied away, for example, from the implications of his doctrine of ressentiment, or the Overman. Sooner or later a responsive spirit will take up the philosophical discourse. Wagner, however, is an artist, a composer of music-dramas. To get at his world view we must garner elements from his own biography and his personal statements, secondly, from his theoretical writing, a syntactical labyrinth yet packed with minotauric concepts, thirdly, from the actual works. It could be argued that the works should speak for themselves. They do. But the age he lived through, with all its reversals of political impulse, with its narrowing dialectic between revolution and imperialism, as well as his own highly significant role as a revolutionary as famous to the European secret police as he was later to become to its new educated classes, all enrich and thicken the texture of significances and values as they emerge, contradict and collide. In the later – never the last – analysis we can discern a private resolution of his internal being and his mortal life before the cosmic nature of existence and a temperate but unyielding revolutionary conviction that the future would accomplish what his times had failed to honour. Our opposition to the critics is not inspired by unthinking partisan loyalty, that is to enter into the dialectical method of ressentiment, which Nietzsche has warned us to avoid for it is the ideology of the slaves. Wagner's work simply has to be taken for itself. His works are musico-dramatic creations whose impact on us will either give us vision and values or will fail to do so. Assessment somehow implies your superiority over the object of study and Wagner's works are not made to be examined like a thesis or a micro-organism. Wagner saw his kindred spirits as Shakespeare and Beethoven, in this he was not immodest but honest to himself and his true nature. The only other figure who can be evoked alongside him is Aeschylus, perhaps even closer to him than these two. To know Wagner one must have the intellectual courage to go where he goes and be led into his world of myth and legend and folk memory, and more importantly, one must learn to use the ear as an instrument of the psyche and read the aural mathematics of his musical theorems which describe action and self and motivation. We must learn from his quite magical scoring to read the hidden meanings of people's words under stress as Siegfried learned to read them from the forest Songbird, which Wagner himself had noted down on his Alpine walks. Always and in every situation however fraught with personal intensity and human passion we are brought into contact with the unending music of nature itself which continues around the human drama sometimes in harmony sometimes in tragic or ironic counterpoint to it. Dawn which is an almost unbearable anguish for Tristan and Isolde is an intoxicating and erotic awakening for Brünn-hilde and Siegfried. The elements participate in the action of existence in a crucial way, Brünnhilde in her ring of fire, the Rhine Daughters swirling in the depths of the river, Erda rising from the depths of the earth, the storm swirling around the Walküre. Rivers and mountains, gardens and forest are the settings in which the human species plays out its most urgent political struggles and its most intimate yearnings. It is like travel, if you do not like to travel you are not going to enjoy Japan. The discovery of Wagner is the discovery of a whole continent and its heart is what Nietzsche described as 'the colossal four-towered edifice of Nibelungen'.[1]

The Ring was both conceived and created during a time of tremendous upheaval and in which all previous values were being questioned. It is very important that in our study we bear in mind two perspectives. One, that of a lucid and informed creative intellect working with the world-view, however radical, shared by those around him, and two, that of the visionary artist who sees beyond the locked dialectics of his epoch and assesses existence with completely new and as yet undefined concepts and even values which await the future to be unlocked. This is very much Wagner's situation, and at times, dilemma. Being who he was he had access to all the most questing spirits of his age, and his wide range of acquaintances and intellectual friendships was unequalled and indeed exposes the domestic perspective of other composers. On the one hand he had to grasp at whatever formulations spoke to him in even a relevant way, let alone an illuminating one, and on the other he had to go outside his own art and try to formulate in involuted prose the glimpses he had of the future possibilities of the human species.

Much is made of the influence of Schopenhauer on the Ring, although calmer and more serious analysts have now assessed that the encounter with the Schopenhauerian concepts of the will came later and Wagner grasped at them to confirm elements of an already existing political vision. They can only be discerned overtly in the moral ambience of his last work, Parsifal, and may be what lend to that complex work an at times lugubrious mood. Others grasp at Feuerbach as the Ring's ideologue, with more persuasion. Yet it must not be forgotten that as well as what we may define as the passive philosophical scene in which he lived there also was the active one much of which occurred on his journeys and the rest in the salon of Wahnfried, his Bayreuth home, and earlier at Triebschen.

The Ring is inescapably a political work and as such it therefore has a philosophical foundation. It is not necessary that this be so in a systemic pattern. It needs not and cannot be located firmly in Schopenhauer's system despite certain ambiguous elements that can be identified. At the same time it is self-defined as not being Hegelian, for example, or Lutheran, however, the value structure which does sustain the vast work is philosophical and has its own inner logic and identity.

People are nowadays warned in ominous and

emotional terms against any tendency to think on a global scale about 'world problems' and even more so about 'world solutions', ironically, just at the moment in history when it is absolutely obligatory to confront historical imperatives and global strategies on a large scale, for the world itself has been structured through technology into a networked system and that system must be manipulated, controlled and understood if we are to avoid either tyranny or world destruction. This rejection of over-view is against the whole foundational thinking of western civilisation, for it underlies the scientific discourse and the Kantian model which was offered to allow the transformation of society to go ahead without the hindrance of a methodology inhibited by metaphysical critique. The ongoing redefinition of these primal models on which technology was based and evolved thus left room for a deeper and deeper probing into the nature of Being itself and therefore of the destiny of the human creature thrown-into-the-world.

Thus the critique of the societal system and the critique of man the moral animal go hand in hand and this has been the fundamental philosophical dialogue of western society giving it its particular identity, indicating more and more technical command marred by a more and more acute existential dilemma of both meaning and bearability – simply being able to tolerate the difficult fact of existence.

When we examine Wagner's private life of intellectual friendship, it would be far from true to imagine that he spent all his energy on his various amorous adventures and his equally imaginative plots for financial support. His library alone remains one of the most fascinating of the great libraries in preservation, but what interests us more is the long series of exchanges that took place in front of its books and in those long walks by the lakes of Switzerland and the woods of Bavaria. His wife's remarkable Diary gives many confirmatory glimpses into these evenings, and it is moving to read of the high quality of intellectual and philosophical questing that these friends shared in those difficult days.

In his own thinking, out beyond the formulations, however radical, of his contemporaries, Wagner had come to formulate a dual problem facing mankind. The basis of the crisis was not one thing, one irrational function in a logical system which implied a path to auto-destruction, but that that one irrational function which revealed itself in the societal structure in turn had its basis in the identity of man. Thus, he saw us faced with a dual task. It was necessary to dismantle the societal system or super-structure which had imposed itself on previous 'natural' systems, and also to dismantle the self-system or infrastructure of the individual identity since it is that which licenses the world system to continue, and this due to that self's robotic condition from which it must be freed before it can make the act of liberation which will in turn destroy the state system. The irrational function within the societal system which was the instrument which upheld tyrannical statism was usury. Destroy usury and you destroy the unjust structuralist state. But this cannot happen unless you de-motivate man from robotic continuity. This can only be done by creating a free man. It is this theme that vibrates and evolves and is so profoundly meditated throughout the Ring, and aspects of it vibrate through all the Master's works. As he unearthed the deep undertow of psychic forces which subverted historical growth and evolution he saw more clearly the true quality of civic harmony. In other words, the psychic insights of Tristan allow the celebration of social well-being which illuminates his radiant Meistersinger.

In all of Wagner's life there was one man who deeply understood this visionary and dual character of Wagner's thinking. That was Friedrich Nietzsche, the philosopher of the age and as much a man of the future as Richard Wagner. History has enshrined a titanic enmity between these two dominant figures of their century based on a series of facts and facts withheld alongside a simple acceptance of Nietzsche's version of the break and his more and more hostile declarations in his final years as insanity broke in on him. This combined with a few legends to embroider the momentous turn-about and the official version of the Wagner-Nietzsche antagonism was complete.

It must be remembered however that Nietzsche was at Bayreuth with the Wagners for the famous first performance of the cycle in 1876. Recent scholarship has established that in October 1876 the Wagners and Nietzsche were taking a pleasant walk together in Sorrento. We also know that the philosopher's first reaction to the text of Parsifal was positive. He also penned one of its most famous tributes. What has been unearthed in new research is that the irreparable break between the two is the result of a most unfortunate and unpardonable intimate breach of privacy between Wagner and Nietzsche's doctor about Nietzsche's sexual activities. Nietzsche loved Wagner and was in love with Cosima, such a betrayal and such an assessment by his beloved Master was too much for the highly tuned and vulnerable psyche of Nietzsche. The famous anti-Wagnerian position he created was a complete turn around from his deepest views on his friend, but friendship's laws are implacable and never more so than when broken. That is why while Nietzsche sneered and mocked more and more in these last years of public writing, Wagner remained silent, a fitting nobility after his ignoble indiscretion.

Nietzsche, being Nietzsche, nevertheless has made some of his barbs stick, others are unfortunate and always seemed, even before we knew what we now know, not to contain the usual scything exactness of Nietzschean diagnosis, but rather an unworthy vulgarity. Our purpose in touching on this is to put in perspective the fact that during all the long period of Wagner's late creativity up until he was half way through Parsifal, his last work, Nietzsche was an intimate friend of the Wagners and spent many nights with them, lived at Wahnfried, and shared the southern holidays which were then as now the necessary winter fare of German intellectuals. In as much as Nietzsche expressed his inner visions to anyone he must have opened his intellect and heart to Wagner. Wagner was a notorious discourser but he also knew how to listen with enormous active enthusiasm, and he expected conversations to be on that high level that had nurtured him all his life in the company of men as mixed as Baudelaire, Berlioz, Gottfried Keller, and Bakunin – and there were many more. It is not some kind of cosmic accident that the Ring is, more than anything else, a Nietzschean work. If we are to 'situate' the Ring philosophically anywhere it is as a complex working of the great Nietzschean themes. And it was the result of their deep and private connection with each other. Nietzsche too in that sense is a Wagnerian, but not, of course in the sense of those first dreadful worshippers who hung around Bayreuth, and he was the first and the most effective rejector of them, but rather in the sense of those capable of recognising what the composer meant.

We will have to examine at length the outcome of that intellectual friendship, and while it was surely central to the outcome of Wagner's created and imagined world, it was not the only friendship or direct influence to nourish his emerging world-view. Nietzsche had been a Wagnerian since hearing the music in 1861, but he was not to have his first fateful meeting with the Master until November of 1868. From then the great friendship was to flourish and mutually inspire them until the abrupt and shocking 'betrayal' and separation in Wagner's last days, ending without even a parting due to their own individual and different experiences of shame.

In 1849 Wagner, with Lohengrin scored but unperformed and with the Ring conceived and its last poem of Götterdämmerung written, was living through the most crucial and tempestuous events of his time. He found himself at the heart both of the Dresden Uprising and also the circles of the radical ideologues who were its virtual authors. It should not be forgotten by armchair musicologists that living out a radical struggle and actively risking life and limb in order to change society within a social context of enormous confusion, violence, and incoherence is not the same as holding liberal ideas counted as superior to those of extremists or even holding radical ideas without needing to act politically. Nor should it be forgotten that the knowledge gained by political activism is not the same as a body of opinions forged by thinking and reading the press.

It was in the midst of this fruitless and premature turmoil that was the Dresden Uprising that Wagner met with the renowned anarchist and revolutionary, Mikhail Bakunin. This brief and intense friendship which was to last only a few weeks, during which the two men were inseparable, was nevertheless to leave a lasting impression on Wagner all his life. For one thing he realised that Bakunin was the very type of the revolutionary, ruthless, free and without ties, while Wagner was the very type of the artist, committed to revolution but needing social harmony, equilibrium, and withdrawal to create his works. In this they were complementary, so different and so in harmony, both longing for the destruction of the terrible corrupt edifice of late christian imperialism, Wagner in his turn with a longer view than Bakunin dreading that christian tyranny might be followed by its partner jewish tyranny. In this he was nearer to Nietzsche than Bakunin.

It is so important for the modern mind to grasp that the events of the nineteenth century had produced a dialectic – and Nietzsche correctly saw that that dialectic could change nothing for the methodology itself, let alone the contents of the dialectic, was the stuff of tyranny. Thus the dialectic would remove the masters and the slaves would rule but they would not be masters but only slaves in power driven by ressentiment. The great writers and artists of that epoch passionately desired transformative change, indeed revolution. The then current events however expressed the concept of revolution inside a dialectic. It is as if the vision of revolution was 'stolen' by the political dialectic and used while in fact it was setting up not the revolution that would abolish the existing power structures but simply arranging for them to change hands. Out with dynastic rule and out with the christian ethos – that was what was set up and achieved in these last years of the nineteenth century and first years of the twentieth. The great giants of the time had hoped for, and some worked for, a much deeper change which would have been in reality revolutionary.

Beethoven considered Plato's Republic to be 'the model for all governments to set up in every part of the world' and his disillusion with Napoleon was his recognition that he was not a platonist but yet another puppet with dynastic pretensions. His Ninth Symphony whenever it was heard represented a hymn to just this deep revolution and was recognised as such so that when Wagner conducted it in the middle of the Dresden upheavals Bakunin was moved to announce to those present that if everything perished they must preserve this great masterpiece. It was a call to a new society beyond the tyrannical statist structure in whose thrall modern man was being destroyed. Wagner's renowned letter of May 1849 which contains the phrase 'and so I say goodbye to revolution'[2] was followed by a vehement declaration from Zürich at the end of the same year, 'It's my job to make revolution wherever I go!'[3]

What Wagner had understood by his active role in the Dresden revolt was something intrinsic to the political personality. At the same time he had no doubt that there was both a pedagogic and an artistic role that had to be played and which perhaps only he could play.

We are left with a picture of how a creative

intellect forms its world-view. There is what is available of ideological material written by contemporaries, there is the direct impact of dynamic exchange of ideas against a background of immediate active experience of political struggle, and there is lastly the personal and inner vision and reflection on these themes some of which may be clumsily put forward in polemical texts, and then all these three elements can be gathered and gone beyond in the metaphoric language of dramatic and musical expression that was Wagner's particular medium of communication. Nor should it be forgotten that with the coming of late and unprecedented fame the composer never ceased to exchange ideas with the most fascinating and original intellects of Europe many of whom came to him in Bayreuth while others met with him in Paris, Zürich, or on his summer sojourns.

As far as Americanism, that is constitutional statism, was concerned Wagner categorically rejected it as simply a modern version of dynastic statism. Communism as an idea naturally appealed to him, but as a doctrine and worked out theory there is absolutely no evidence that he ever met it. Certainly as we now know it he would have opposed it utterly, since it in turn is another statism and nowhere calls in moral question the usurious principle that underlies corrupt power. Recent attempts to subsume the Wagnerian world-view under marxism either in theory or in theatrical production have all failed. Wagner's critique of modern society – and modern society itself was emerging in full contour during his lifetime – went much deeper. Capital is not the problem in the Ring. What is at issue is the life-project itself. Underlying his politique is his philosophical position and it is not an ad hoc life-raft hastily nailed together from bits of Feuerbach and Proudhon and finally bailed out by the Schopenhauerian ladle. His political viewpoint is in disarray and sometimes dishonest – the radical thinker so ahead of his time that he must depend on the subsidies of a demented monarch – but his philosophical foundations are powerful, original and personal. Based on an enquiring and respectful involvement with the ancients – Greek tragedy and Germanic myth – he looked for those elements which would allow the human project to survive and also confront its own identity. The peace he makes between himself as artist and as politician is to be found in the Meistersinger, as we will see. For the artist, humble and pessimistic resignation. For the politician, civic celebration and gratitude for German humanness. The truth is that Wagner was far nearer to Goethe than he ever was to Schopenhauer, who in turn had not the faintest idea what Wagner was trying to do.

Wagner the Goethean has still to be explored, but there is no doubt that his musings on Faust and his concept of an open theatre in which people participated in the action of that play were enlaced with his own idea and need for a civic playhouse especially for his works.

Wagner is not a politician, but he is political. Wagner is not a philosopher, but he has a philosophy. Wagner is an artist and he is very careful to define his role not through any modesty – he knew his own genius and had no doubt of it – but because he considered the role of artist to be of supreme importance for mankind. As he wrote in his introduction to Art and Revolution:

> 'I believed in the Revolution, and in its unrestrainable necessity, with certainly no greater immoderation than Carlyle: only I also felt that I was called to point out to it the way of rescue. It was far from my intention to define the new life that ought to emerge from a false world in a new political order but I felt the urge to sketch the outlines of the artwork which should rise from the ruins of false art.'[4]

He wrote that in 1872. It is absurd to imagine that Wagner was devoid of intellect simply because he expressed his ideas in tortuous prose. He possessed one of the greatest and most far-seeing intellects of all time and his expression of that intellect is to be found first and foremost in his music-dramas, and then in those theoretical writings which are the very necessary preparation and clearing-house for those visionary works. So significant are these theoretical writings that we may say that they have not yet been examined in a constructive critical light, although it is beginning to happen. Many surprises await those strong intellects prepared to cut through the syntactically clogged prose to the extraordinary wealth of ideas embedded in it. Wagner's analysis of language and its roots and its relation to sung speech can only now be given a fair hearing since we live in an age that has both 'discovered' the importance of language and has already passed through the disillusionment of a pseudo-science that tried to lay bare the roots and function of language with a methodology pretending to be scientific. Wagner in his theoretical writings came straight to the heart of the matter when he insisted that basic human communication has in it, right at the beginning, feelings.

'Tone-speech is the beginning and end of word-speech, as the feeling is the beginning and end of the understanding, as myth is the beginning and end of history, the lyric beginning and end of poetry.'[5] After the failure of modern linguistics this is easy for us to understand and also a radical concept. When he goes on to say that feeling 'has escaped from absolute intellectual-speech by hiding in absolute tone-speech – our contemporary music,'[6] we recognise immediately his idea, one that seemed quite crazy over a hundred years ago, as did the, to us quite beautiful, song of the Rhine Daughters with its alliterative yet wordless poetry.

When Wagner talks about 'the sensuous substance of our roots of speech' he is not merely raising a musical issue, he is touching on a theme to us that lies at the crucial centre of our contemporary discourse.

Thus it was, equipped as best he was able, that Wagner set out to explore a life-time's set of themes that utilised ancient pagan and christian myths, that evoked medieval and ancient worlds. Within these realms he set about making his bridge to the future, his contribution to the deep revolution he politically knew had not even begun but which had to begin if mankind was to have a future at all. Wagner's pessimism is not resignation like Schopenhauer's, it is nihilistic in the constructive and renewing sense that Nietzsche's is. Most ironic of fates, but what is needed for a profound appreciation of Wagner is an act of complete de-mythologising, not, that is, in the usual sense of stripping away the myth to get to the reality, but rather in stripping away the vivid realism to get to the meanings. This is not to imply approval of the in vacuo productions at Bayreuth which followed World War Two, although if they had not been so presented Bayreuth might have been destroyed, or the hopeless inadequacy of trying to submit the whole of the Ring to a Jungian mapping of Richard Wagner's apparently completely Jungian psyche. What we are required to do is meet Wagner in his vivid immediacy and recognise that he was in his art a futurist reaching out to us and not at all addressing his nineteenth century bourgeois audience and even less catering to the romantic maunderings of his mad monarchic banker. We must meet his challenge when he wrote to Theodor Uhlig: 'Revolution alone can give me the artists and audiences I need.'[7] He said he would convey in his works the meaning of their revolution in its noblest form. Then, he insisted, there would be an audience which could understand him, for his contemporaries could not.

To be specific, critics and producers stubbornly take Tannhäuser to be a completely christian medieval romance, a piece of Gothic to take its place alongside William Morris prints and Victorian nostalgia. Wagner himself writes in 'A Communication to My Friends': 'How absurd then must those critics seem to me, who, drawing all their wit from modern wantonness, insist on reading into my Tannhäuser a specifically christian and im-potently pietistic drift!'[8]

The need is not to locate the action of the Ring in science-fiction settings or overload it with psycho-analytic symbols, both Wagner's sense of the future and his understanding of the psyche transcend these genres radically. The need is to think about the Wagnerian vision and see it as well as hear it, grasp it as well as surrender to it.

2

HIS WORKS

Strictly speaking the complete Wagnerian corpus begins with Lohengrin but mention should be made of the two works in which he first touched one of his essential themes, and in which he first heard to his own satisfaction a sonority from the orchestra, a first attempt at sung speech, and most importantly the first grasp of the value of dramatic structure in determining the musical expression itself. The first, of course, was The Flying Dutchman. Its significance for us is the importance which its composer placed on the person of Senta who gives her life to release the unfortunate sailor from his endless travel. The work ends with the two in apotheosis, very much in the genre he was so soon to abandon, grand opera.

Wagner was unable to realise in Senta what he later understood as his vision of women. But he had 'thought' her, he had reached out beyond the operatic convention and taken strength from the myth, in this case so fragile, to allow him to glimpse woman in a new way. He explains in 'A Communication to my Friends':

> '... she is no longer the home-tending Penelope of Ulysses, as courted in the days of old, but the quintessence of womankind; and yet the still unmanifest, the longed-for, the dreamt-of, the infinitely womanly woman – let me out with it in one word: THE WOMAN OF THE FUTURE.'[9]

Now this simply did not make sense in 1851 when he wrote it, nor did it to the early Wagnerians, it shocked Newman who basically thought his brain was deformed and yet spent a whole lifetime writing about him, and Shaw discreetly avoided the issue, despite his own heroic attempts to inform the age he lived in that women were now due recognition at last.

While Wagner stands utterly alone in the musical and post-operatic world he created he has in the theatre a man who came very near to him both in his primary human concerns and in his central understanding that what man and women were would constitute the basis for society not structuralist authority. Henrik Ibsen. His work moves between heroic myth and intimate psychologism in just the way that the composer's does. Hedda and Nora may seem far from Brünnhilde and Fricka yet what they share is a new perspective which sees them experiencing themselves as women for themselves and not merely as warm mannequins decorating the arena of male drama.

With Tannhäuser comes the first Wagnerian statement. It is formal, structurally filled with traditional elements and yet already we are in the world of Wagner, in the tension between resonant but distant social struggle and close intolerable personal contradictions which must be resolved. He has taken the first step in projecting his personal vision. He has let us taste the social identity, however formally, in procession and choral statement, and at the same time participate in a personal crisis which is nothing less than a man and a woman coming to selfhood through contemplating not the other, but the self in the other.

Again the woman saves the man yet this time

the woman is deeper, more complex than Senta, she is far from being a salvation machine for the male psyche. The intriguing element in Tannhäuser is that the author has, as it were, split the female identity into two. On the one side is Venus, who rules on the unambiguously named Venusberg, where sexual delight and enjoyment are the unique nourishment. The dramatic fact on which the action turns is that Tannhäuser wants something more out of life. He wants something to happen, even pain in order to go beyond the state the Venusberg can offer him. Elisabeth, on her side, is aroused by the restless yearning of Tannhäuser, and through him enters into a different dimension of life:

> 'Gefühle, die ich nie empfunden!
> Verlangen, das ich nie gekannt!'

> (Sensations I have never felt.
> Longings I have never known).

It is Tannhäuser's ambiguous view of Venus and Elisabeth that gives the action its central conflict. While he himself longs for the real encounter with Elisabeth it is as artist and poet that he cannot resist confirming the splendour of the Venusberg. And in this formal confrontation of Tannhäuser's poetique and that of the Landgrave's knights we also have the first essay in the role of the poet-artist in relation to his society. It is a first draft of what will become Wagner's sublime masterpiece, Die Meistersinger von Nürnberg. But the latter, coming after great struggles and enriched by the eventful life of its creator will see a different kind of outcome to the song competition, a deeper more philosophical friendship than the formal courtly one between Tannhäuser and Wolfram, a full and confident confirmation of the union between man and woman, and most importantly, a noble and resigned artist whose deep love of the Volk in the end is more important than the world of the imagination that is the Venusberg. But of that later.

The work ends in a certain confusion through which we glean both the death of Elisabeth and the answer to her prayer in the saving of Tannhäuser. His pilgrimage to Rome had been a failure with the Pope cynically declaring that he could not be saved unless his pilgrim's staff burst into flower. Since this is exactly what happens it is clear that we have moved into a post-christian world where people save each other and the official religion does not come to grips with the passions by which people live and die.

With the score of Tannhäuser completed Wagner took the cure at Marienbad. It was there, taking the waters that so much of his future lay in wait for him. There, he read about Parsifal, prepared a first scenario for Die Meistersinger, and one day leapt out of his bath after only a few minutes of the prescribed hour with a wonderful new idea. That idea was Lohengrin. It was 1845.

Lohengrin, the first work in the great Wagner canon, is linked directly to its last, Parsifal. The cyclic pattern of his mature consciousness is in appropriate form and confirms incidentally his own world-view. Yet while in the early work, complex only in its psychology not its framework, christianity is set against paganism in a symbolism that sets light against darkness, by the time Wagner reaches the end of his own journey, the Grail of Parsifal, despite all the christian trimmings is resolutely stripped of all christian meanings, blood sacrifice, redemption through death, sacramental drinking, all are gone at the court of the Grail, in its place is brotherhood, compassion, and serenity.

Wagner had a long and medically heart-breaking path to explore before this final personal peace that he was to achieve. Just as his first attempt at a personal vision forced him through his own experience and through the common prejudice of his epoch to see in women an irremediable split between whore and wife, so too in Lohengrin, his first mature work, he was to present the idea of the couple, of the man and woman as partners, as a tragically unattainable dream. Lohengrin is often presented as the ultimate and absolute Romantic opera. Certainly it is an opera, although the composer has already at this stage discovered a brilliant command over his textual material so that he has found a means to weave together recitative material with melodic phrasing. In Lohengrin he is only a step away from that all but complete abandoning of the aria-recitative split which was to mark his great masterpieces. In the sense that its tragic outcome leaves one still enthralled by the impossible yearnings of its central figures, it is a Romantic opus. In Tristan there is a sense of its protagonists having utterly successfully worked out the desired destiny and its function is not to arouse in us that yearning for it has been exhausted and expunged from our psyches in such a way that it categorically lies beyond the romantic experience. Nevertheless, one can already find in Lohengrin if not a post-romantic dimension at least the author's subversive intent, and most certainly his desire to move beyond the impasse created by his drama.

The story briefly is that Lohengrin, Knight of the Grail comes to the camp of the German King to help a woman in trouble. The army is marching East against invading forces but the King is troubled at the disunity in the land of Brabant where they are. Elsa has been falsely accused of killing her brother and plotting for the throne, an affair in fact in the hands of the dark-couple, Telramund and Ortrud, the pagans. Elsa immediately falls in love with Lohengrin of whom she has dreamed and all is set both to exonerate her and for them to marry. The intolerable element around which the tragedy revolves, is that Lohengrin has set as condition to their marriage the promise that she will not ask him his name and thus force him to reveal his identity. Thanks to the clever manipulation of Ortrud, Elsa finds herself insisting on his name and the opera ends with the resolution of everyone's problems but the destruction of poor Elsa. When he tells the assembled company he is Lohengrin of the Grail, son of Parsifal, the people lament his departure, Elsa's brother is transformed back to life, but she dies in her brother's arms as the glorious figure of the knight in shining armour sails away drawn by his emblematic swans, the dove of the Grail's peace hovering over the tragic scene.

Wagner has, of course, immortalised the ancient legend with his rich and stately music. It is not moving but it is wrapped in a cloak of harmonies that enchant the listener to such an extent that if one did not know what lay ahead from the same pen one would make greater claims for the work and not accept the place it is normally assigned.

What is of interest to us here however is his insight into the human situation of men and women. While his friends understandably complained about the coldness of Lohengrin in denying Elsa simply because she wants to know his name, Wagner with all his sense of dramatic rightness refused to change that very element in the legend that had attracted him in the first place. He is not right because of the lofty spiritual meaning of Lohengrin's undertaking of anonymity, but he is right in his own incapacity to see beyond the dichotomy created between man with a project and woman who wished man as hers. Since that is the contract, it is better rejected, he seems to say. But as yet he cannot see his way forward to another man-woman contract that will remove the conditional basis of encounter.

At the same time, because of his artistic integrity, he is able to make a psychological leap of recognition. It is in this meaning that we can perceive a depassement of the Romantic dilemma, of which women are the undoubted victims. Let us read Wagner's own words on the matter, words which at the time caused enormous confusion, but which to our modern awareness are so clear:

'Elsa is the Unconscious, the Undeliberate
into which Lohengrin's conscious, deliberate

being yearns to be redeemed; but this yearning, again, is itself the unconscious, undeliberate necessity in Lohengrin, whereby he feels himself akin to Elsa's being. Through the capability of this 'unconscious consciousness' such as I myself now felt alike with Lohengrin, the nature of woman also came to an ever clearer understanding in my inner mind... Elsa, this glorious woman, before whom Lohengrin must vanish, for reason that his own specific nature could not understand her – I found her NOW: and the random shaft that I had shot towards the treasure dreamt but hitherto unknown, was my own Lohengrin, whom now I must give up as lost, to track more certainly the footsteps of that TRUE WOMANHOOD, which should one day bring to me and all the world redemption, after man's egoism, even in its noblest form, had shivered into self-crushed dust before her – Elsa the woman – woman hitherto un-understood by me, and understood at last – that most positive expression of the purest instinct of the senses – made me a revolutionary at one blow.'[10]

He further remarked about Ortrud: 'Ortrud is a

woman who does not know love. Politics are her essence. The political man is repulsive but the political woman is horrible and it is this horror I had to represent.'[11] Already there in the mid-nineteenth century he had recognised that the opposite of the woman-as-victim as understood both by bourgeois existence and also by its false doctrine of escape, Romanticism, was not the deceptively simple act of turning the woman into a man and giving her man's project alongside other men while denying her intrinsic identity and uniqueness. He had seen, as his writing confirms, that woman had a particular spiritual significance that had to interact with that of men, and it was this insight he deliberately declared that transformed him into a revolutionary. His great insight is not simply that the nature of the state is the result of the nature of the individual but that the basis of society must cease to be that of man who is only part of 'the purely human'.

The other element that must be taken into account is the German dimension which reverberates throughout all of Wagner's work with the exception of Tristan. Here, in this first of his great works the connection between the political background and the personal drama is very formal and even stilted yet it gives a depth to the characters and sets an atmosphere of urgency among them before the main crisis declares itself with the arrival of the Grail Knight. As the opera opens, the German King Henry is discovered on the banks of the River Scheldt near Antwerp. He is there to strengthen the unity of the people and prepare for an assault against the invading hordes from the East. The words spoken by the German King were controversial and even dangerous when they were first heard, in 1919 they again had an important significance to the German people after the humiliating Versailles treaty, and an even greater one as the German Reich found itself facing Russia in 1939. To the modern German whose country then suffered division these words maintain their relevance and power to move the listener.

'Soll ich euch erst der Drangsal Kunde sagen,
die deutsches Land so oft aus Osten traf?'

(Need I tell you of the affliction
so often wrought upon German soil from
the East?)

We will examine more fully this vital dimension of the genius of Wagner, his Germanness, which weighs and empowers his work with an added vitality and vision which truly makes it universal. Once we have examined his works more fully, and examined the Ring, we can then return to this theme better able to gauge its importance to his art and to us.

Der Ring des Nibelungen, Wagner's masterwork, was written over a period of almost twenty-five years, and before that was meditated on and then sketched out both in language and notation over a period of years. Its ultimate gestation involved a significant gap in mid-stream during which its author composed two great music dramas, each of which alone would guarantee its creator immortality, one totally subjective and a study in depth-psychology and the other an enormous civic panorama celebrating the virtues of the fundamental town life that underlies western civilisation. He then returned to finish Siegfried and write the final drama, Götterdämmerung, completing the whole vast trilogy and prefatory drama on the 21st of November, 1874. On the 4th of October, 1848 he had drafted an essay entitled 'The Saga of the Nibelungen' which was the first outline of what was to become the Ring. It was later published under the title of 'The Myth of the Nibelungen'.

Recent Wagnerian scholarship has finally eliminated the supercilious view that somehow Wagner had no deep knowledge of his subject and simply scratched together a version of an existing legend altering it where it suited him for his own purposes.

We now know the remarkable and scholarly research that went into the preparatory stages which culminated in the various drafts and final text of the Ring. The wedding together of various strands of the legend, the use of different sources, the astonishingly harmonious invention in Rheingold of new material, all indicate Wagner's serious background work and his mastery of the mythic roots of his music-drama. Not only had Wagner gone into the farthest reaches of the Germanic people's legendary past but he had also drawn on ancient history so that the resonance of his work was sustained not just by its mythic basis but by its being deeply embedded in the past of his Volk. Part of the enormous universal impact of the work is due particularly to this specific Germanness of the root material. By being true to 'there' it somehow is true 'everywhere', and so it is that modern men and women can enter a world drawn from an ancient and specific mythology of gods and dragons and dwarfs only to discover themselves in an utterly enthralling encounter with modern technology, statism, psychology and the future of the human race.

Nietzsche's dictum from his notes in 'The Will to Power' (602) could be taken as the epigraph for this unique and enormous artistic achievement. He said, 'We have art in order not to perish from the truth.'[12] It is also relevant to his next work.

It was before confronting the crucial and pivotal Act Three of Siegfried that the composer interrupted his magnum opus to create Tristan and Meistersinger. Do not forget this vital aspect of Wagner's psyche – he had all his basic artistic material almost from the beginning. That Lohengrin is the son of Parsifal is in itself perfectly harmonious with the cyclical view of existence which he himself is contemplating.

Thus the first thing we must say about Tristan is that he began to write it because it was time for him to write it. He needed it and the compulsion is so strong that it is almost as if, too, it needed him, and had to declare itself. With Tristan we reach into the deepest depths of Wagner's being, but also at the same time into the modern age. I do not mean the nineteenth century, and even less do I refer to the so-called Romantic Agony, an invention of critics, not artists. No word will lead us further from Wagner than the word romantic and it is so clear why his works receive this label that it renders the act of labelling in itself banal. To suggest he really embodied its opposite would be equally foolish. To penetrate into the depths of the Wagnerian world and selfhood a more powerful act of the imagination and the intellect is required.

The stunning fact is that here in the realm of

the inner self Wagner moved with absolute confidence both as to what he wanted to say and how he wanted to express it. It is not some haunted piece of free association, it has not the slightest suggestion of openness, or improvisation. It could not be further from the spirit of Lautreamont's Maldoror. It is constructed of quite new musical material and method, its orchestration ushers in the future of modern music. Its tonality, sonority and flow, all its technical originality remain tautly circumscribed by a ruthless narrative control of the material, and after the titanic wrestling with antique sources for the Ring, here the Master forges from the legend a perfectly wrought story, as tragically complete as the Celtic serpent which emblematically devours its tail.

'In perfect confidence,' Wagner writes, 'I plunged into the inner depths of soul events, and from the innermost centre of the world, I fearlessly built up its outward form. A glance at the size of this poem will show you at once that I have taken the detailed precision which the historical poet is obliged to employ when explaining the outer coherences of dramatic actions, to the detriment of the clear exposition of the inner motives, and dared to apply it to the latter alone. Life and death, the whole meaning and existence of the outer world, here hang on nothing but the inner movements of the soul, the whole decisive action materialises when the innermost soul demands it, and comes forward to reveal itself with the very shape predicted within the inner shrine.'[13]

What temerity one must have to imagine one can write a Jungian or a Freudian analysis of a Wagner music drama when the artist himself is so supremely aware of what he is doing and is consciously moving and expounding a psychic thesis! It is not 'in' his theoretical writings that Wagner reveals his mastery of his psychic material but in the works themselves, so structured and so disciplined and so completely new in their language of communication, it is against these rocks that the waves of criticism are dashed.

So supremely confident is Wagner in Tristan of his music's capacity to express all and everything, he leaves very little to the text to expound. It is necessary simply to move the inexorable narration of the spare and precipitate events to their final conclusion. In the Meistersinger which is a kind of creative opposite, the text dominates the nevertheless sublime music. There we need it and cannot do without it. In Tristan it is merely a formality. Yet in a way the genius of the text is that it all lies in the title. 'Tristan und Isolde'. The tragedy reveals itself openly in the text – the intolerable otherness which prevents the bliss being the bliss of life. Isolde sings:

Doch uns're Liebe,	But this our love
heißt sie nicht Tristan	Is it not called Tristan
und – Isolde?	and – Isolde?
Dies süße Wörtlein: und,	this sweet little word 'and'
was es bindet,	binding as it does
der Liebe Bund,	love's union,
wenn Tristan stürb',	would death not destroy it
zerstört' es nicht der Tod?	were Tristan do die?

Tristan replies:

Was stürbe denn Tod,	What could death destroy
als was uns stört,	but what impedes us,
was Tristan wehrt,	that hinders Tristan
Isolde immer zu lieben,	from loving Isolde forever,
ewig ihr nur zu leben?	and forever living but
	for her?

Isolde goes on:

Doch dieses Wörtlein: und –	yet this little word 'and' –
wär' es zerstört,	how might it be destroyed
wie anders als	other than
mit Isoldes eignem Leben	with Isolde's own life,
wär' Tristan der Tod gegeben?	if death were to be given
	Tristan?

The great love duet – though this tawdry operatic term has little to do with the overwhelming emotional impact of this long and complex musical encounter – of which these lines are part, ends with the ultimate commitment to the 'love' at the price of their selfhood with the two lovers in a complete delirium of sexual passion:

Both:

Ohne Nennen,	No names,
ohne Trennen,	no parting:
neu' Erkennen,	newly known
neu' Entbrennen;	newly kindled;
endlos ewig,	ever without end,
ein-bewußt;	one consciousness;
heiss erglühter Brust,	supreme joy of love
höchste Liebeslust!	glowing in our breast!

Heidegger in his long two volume meditation on Nietzsche has very pertinent observations germane to our subject. It should be remarked that it is clear from his writings, firstly, that Heidegger does not understand Wagner's music and takes a rather simplistic view of his 'Romanticism', which does not now seem tenable; secondly, he takes Nietzsche at his word in all he writes about Wagner. Apart from the dramatically new viewpoint that has emerged since the analysis of the correspondence between Wagner and Nietzsche's doctor which indicates that the basis of the split was highly personal and not ideological at all, it must also be allowed that Nietzsche harboured a deep envy of his Master. He himself does write about the necessary rejection of one's master if one is to emerge in full self-hood, but in his own case this emergence is far from being in good faith. Not only was his attachment to Wagner ambiguous and unclear, while expressed intellectually in the early writings which laud the genius of the composer, it was never expressed existentially, and remained haltingly insecure as letters and domestic incidents in the Wagner household reveal. So, while Heidegger separates Wagner from these observations he makes on the philosopher we can now see that the two men were after all very close to each other.

'Nietzsche recognises rapture to be the basic actuality of art.' Heidegger goes on to suggest that art results in the supreme lucidity of Being – and it is here where he defines Wagner's place as simply resulting in a 'visionless tumult' a viewpoint we can whole-heartedly reject, as do the public night after night at the end of the great master-works in the theatre. He continues: 'But in Nietzsche's view that implies at the same time the emergence of the abyss of 'life', of life's essential contradictions, not as moral evil or as something to be negated, but as what is to be affirmed. The 'physiological', the sensuous-corporeal, in itself possesses this beyond-itself.'[14]

No words could be more apposite to a meditation on Tristan. The factor which makes this work so difficult to talk about or think about is that whatever one says remains only after one's overwhelming response to the work in vivo. What must not be forgotten, and perhaps the modern intellect is now trained to this response, is that we submit to the piece as 'a piece of reality' at the same time that we know we are being presented a model by Wagner himself. It is life but it is not life. It is an artistic lie which embodies for us truth.

Heidegger observes, 'Semblance itself is proper to the essence of the real.'[15] This relates to the Nietzsche quotation with which we began our examination of Tristan. What we are confronted with in Tristan is precisely this recognition of the sensuous as having the higher value. It is in the uttermost reaches of the sensuous, sexual and personal obliteration in the orgasmic abandoning of the self in the other, that Wagner, stubbornly rejecting transcendence, finds himself able to offer us a metaphysical statement. It is not Platonic. Wagner's genius for us lies in his insisting that the meaning and the reality are in the experience itself. Yet the outcome of the passion is a cessation of the life which is its basis, and it is here that the lie of the art becomes the truth of life. Heidegger after quoting Nietzsche's 'Semblance as I understand it is the actual and sole reality of things,' (semblance: Schein) continues: 'That should be understood to mean not that reality is something apparent, but that being-real is in itself perspectival, a bringing forward into appearance, a letting radiate; that it is in itself a shining. Reality is radiance.'[16]

Surely this is what happens to us at the end of Tristan, when Isolde experiences her Verklärung, or transfiguration. We recognise the experience. Wagner said he had never known it, some have touched its edges and returned. Hemingway said that people who had been in love were like dead people afterwards. It is not a negation of absolute passion, nor a medical prescription against it. Catharsis is not the therapy of Tristan. We 'live' it, but we survive. Heidegger says: 'Art induces reality, which is in itself a shining, to shine most profoundly and supremely in scintillating transfiguration.'[17]

Nietzsche insisted that his role was the reversal, the turning upside down of Platonism. The highest meaning was to be found not in the super-sensuous world but in sensuality itself. This was the highest reality right in front of us. Thus he moved as it were the frontier of encounter from the dream world and after death to life and therefore also to art. He had observed: 'Art is the proper task of life… art as its METAPHYSICAL activity.'[18] (Will to Power 853).

It is here that Nietzsche's philosophy can be seen in its clarity. For the end of Tristan is nothing other than a manifestation of the meaning of the 'Eternal recurrence of the same' that is one of its key elements. It does not mean as is foolishly supposed by those who have not bothered to read Nietzsche that one loops through the same pattern of actions forever. It means that in the encounter of the moment, before one, like an abyss, is to be found the Eternal, not postponed, but in the encounter with the Now. And since time is finite, curved back on itself, this moment is already passed and has yet to come, it has gone ahead of us, is arriving, not yet born. The instant is the door onto the Absolute without transcendence or delayed encounter, thus Tristan and Isolde in 'their real world', which is our life, a Wagner drama for which we have bought seats, achieve their goal, are fulfilled and transfigured. It is 'ohne End", without end. It is neu' Erkennen, neu' Entbrennen at the same time. Newly known and newly kindled. It is a transfiguration in the deepest metaphysical sense, a shining radiance. Tristan transformed by Isolde in her vision is:

Immer lichter | How he shines
wie er leuchtet | ever brighter

and with that supreme genius of Wagner he crosses over from the lie to the truth of his listeners in the theatre and asks:

Freunde! Seht! | Friends – see!
Fühlt und seht ihr's nicht? | Don't you feel and see it?
Höre ich nur | Do I alone
diese Weise... | Hear this melody...

already, of course, he has us in his thrall – not theirs – and we do not hear the question for by now the glorious sublimity of his orchestra is washing over us so that we have the illusion of this ecstasy, or have this ecstasy, and glimpse in just these final moments what we have been savouring bit by bit throughout the work, some tremendous illumination, one that miraculously does not destroy us.

How Nietzschean it is! And it was the door to Wagner for the young philology student, making such an impact on him that finally he was driven to seek him out. Yet he was to write later with all that ambiguity and imbalance which never left him about all things Wagnerian that he could only read the score of Tristan wearing gloves. That Wagner should have so audaciously taken him at his word, dared what he could not dare and recovered the purely sensual, indeed as he in this admits, the highly sexual, as a realm for the encounter of pure Being, snatching bliss back from a heavenly world postponed into the physical present, and releasing the Dionysiac power of orgasm yet in musical terms – so that the Apollonian discipline of art defends us from madness and annihilation, all this proved to be too much for the sensitive spirit of Nietzsche. He had thought the great thought in his philosophy, and Wagner had lived it, at least in the lie of his art, and, unforgivably it seemed, tasted it in life. How moved he would have been to read his friend's letter to Liszt where he confessed that he himself had never known this all-consuming passion. Or so he said – in fact he had, but it had been a lie, it had been for Isolde.

With Meistersinger another towering achievement of the mature Wagner is set in place. An Olympian triumph acknowledged by his most bitter critics. While this work is also dominated by the Nietzschean world-view here we are in the pure air of the Goethean vision. Both Nietzsche and Wagner were torn in their emotions towards their own people, the former more so than the latter. Yet it is here that Wagner expresses all his great love for Germany in its fullest and richest. Nietzsche's anti-Germanness stems from his own existential alienation and his deep critical diagnosis of the social ills of his time. Wagner's love for Germany, despite his political critique and his antistatist views reaches deeply down into his psyche. As an exile he found himself drawing solace from the medieval legends which form the inspiration for his early works. His massive research before embarking on the Ring gave body and density to his awareness of the meaning of the German tradition. With the Meistersinger he was ready to write his great hymn of praise to the German spirit and character and quality. It was the tribute of a lifetime's love, yet being Wagner he could never embark on anything so univocal in theme as a nationalistic pageant. Further, we should not fail to grasp that his use of the term 'German' is not a nationalistic concept, it is much deeper, more cultural and one may even say purely political. His concept is of the Volk – indeed one protagonist of the work is none other than the Volk. As the title indicates – it is their opera – and not that of any one protagonist.

To those who have been privileged to get to know Wagner somewhat through his work and a knowledge of his life there is always an added dimension of appreciation when listening to the Meistersinger for it is the fullest expression of his generous coming to terms not just with his own art but with life itself. In all his works we are in the

Wagnerian world and he is nowhere present, one simply cannot say that he is Lohengrin or Siegfried or Wotan. Yet in Meistersinger one cannot help feeling he is close. Of course, Sachs expresses one aspect of Mastery and the young Walter, that revolutionary innovator of new forms, another, but only in the sense that they are an intimate 'voice' of the composer, but what we experience is that he is giving us his testament of art and life, truth and illusion. It is to his work like his brother Shakespeare's Tempest in that it represents the poet, his whole world, and his act of making peace with the homeland from which as an artist he has felt so long exiled and misunderstood.

We can find three key subjects dominating this work which he was so affectionately to designate, after all his theories of music-drama, as an opera. The first is 'being German' in the sense of a conscious awareness of embodying the key elements of western civilisation. The second is a meditation on the subject or art and truth, or illusion and reality. The third is the confirmation of civic harmony in a Nürnberg which comes to stand for all mankind. It is clear from this that our 'comic opera' is far from being one – quite apart from the fact that it lasts five hours which is a long time to keep laughing. It is often genuinely funny, but it is full of human emotions, envy, vanity, loneliness, young love, mature love, simple religion, festivity, student life, cultural contest, and the deep glow of mutual acceptance which suffuses the protagonists at the end of the opera, and which gives such radiance to their famous quintet. The ambiguities are honed as finely as the orchestration is expanded fully. Never has the Wagnerian 'sound' been so rich in its harmonies and counterpoint. The famous motives are woven into a carpet of delectable sounds that again and again ravish the listener. The sheer magisterial command of his material is made all the more audacious by the theme, a contest of song by Masters and for Master-hood. Wagner wrote asking us to remember that all this enjoyment was won at a cost.

The work is Goethean in all three of its major themes, but particularly in its affectionate affirmation of Germany. It echoes Faust's words:

'We hold the central position... This land looks only to you. It offers you its flowering wealth. The whole earth is yours but surely you put your home country first.'[19]

Its main theme, the relation between art and reality, between illusion (Wahn) and life, is laid out in complex and openly philosophical language. The irony that gives the work its artistic density is that this theme is explored both within the aesthetic of the Mastersinger's art of songwriting and in the lives of the central characters where love and longing turn the heads and hearts of the otherwise balanced citizens. On the one hand there is the sustaining and vitalising of the art of song, without which the Volk will perish, and on the other hand there is 'Wahn, Wahn! Überall Wahn!' which makes people act without reason in the name of love or violence and even turns the head of the mature Master, Hans Sachs. Thus, the charming love story of the young singer who seeks to be accepted as a Mastersinger is set against human desires and longings that burst out into conflict and anguish in a setting both of civic celebration and disruption. In the end all is harmony, the young lovers are united, the envious artist is reconciled, and the Master is resigned to age and isolation, and all of this is irradiated by the celebration of joy and civic pride which floods over the participants in a warm glow of human affection.

The central theme of the nature of the artistic achievement in turn impinges on the political reality, and it is this verity that gives Meistersinger its force. It is not metaphoric, or mythic, or legendary. We are in medieval Germany with a civic order known and inherited. The central character, Hans Sachs, is based on a known poet of that name, whose face unforgettably stands before us, engraved by Ostendorfer. In this sense, we as audience, part of this culture, are by implication an extension of that singing 'public' onstage, the citizens of Nürnberg.

Heidegger, commenting Nietzsche says:

'The aesthetic state is a doing and perceiving which we ourselves execute. We do not dwell alongside the event as spectators; we ourselves remain within the state. Our Dasein receives from it a luminous relation to beings, the sight in which beings are visible to us. The aesthetic state is the envisionment through which we constantly see, so that everything here is discernible to us. Art is the most visionary configuration of will to power.'[20]

This last phrase is the first of five basic propositions on art which the Freiburg philosopher meditates for us in his examination of Nietzsche to open his thinking to us in our time and for our time. Let us list the Nietzschean principles on art:

1. Art is the most perspicuous and familiar configuration of will to power.
2. Art must be grasped in terms of the artist.

3. Art is the basic occurrence of all beings; to the extent that they are, beings are self-creating, created.
4. Art is the distinctive countermovement to nihilism.
5. Art is worth more than 'the truth'.[21]

In this perspective we can see that Wagner's Meistersinger is not a strange deviation. It is not musically and it is not thematically. It overtly has woven into it textual and musical references to Tristan as well as musical echoes of the Ring. In a sense it is his Testament as has been suggested. The first of the five principles of art informs all Wagner's creative life work. The principle of will-to-power is demonstrated openly and resoundingly in Meistersinger. It forcefully declares that the art of the Mastersingers is of such force that it in turn upholds and defends the society and is that thing which merits such an upholding.

The second principle is confirmed in the consecration by the Mastersingers themselves and by the Volk of Hans Sachs. In the end to confirm him is not merely to confirm his poetic gift but his moral wisdom and noble behaviour. The artistic event reaches beyond the aesthetic not just on one side towards the metaphysical but on the other side towards the social.

In the third principle we see the whole city of Nürnberg, that is the people of our occidental civilisation, taking meaning and life from the celebration of the artistic experience. In this sense it is more important than the religious festival – it is in itself the vehicle for metaphysical meaning. Significantly, the action takes place around the christian holiday of St. Johannes Day, but that is the name of Hans Sachs, and in the end it is HE who is celebrated by the citizens of Nürnberg.

The fourth point is confirmed in that Nietzsche considers the movement of nihilism to be the outcome of the Platonic-Christian negation of the sensuous world in preference for the absent or distant supersensuous world, while art celebrates the sensuous experience. To quote Nietzsche (Will to Power 853 section 11): 'Art as the single superior counterforce against all will to negation of life, art as the anti-christian, anti-buddhist, anti-nihilist par excellence.'[22] Meistersinger is one of the sublime summits of western art and its richly woven musical and theatrical 'reality' fills us with the deepest and most sensuous well-being imaginable. It is precisely for that positive lifeforce that we go to attend Meistersinger, knowing we will emerge radiant with the glow of affirmation.

The last, the metaphysical insight, is the core of Wagner's meditation in Meistersinger. In the end, through Sachs he tells the young rebel Master that he cannot reject their art for his higher 'truth' of love. He needs it to give him his reality. He then goes further and reminds the people, and this includes us, that we cannot live without this either and that this art is what will give 'truth' to our civic values and our whole civilisation, for without it the truths we claim are revealed as false and will be destroyed and over-run by barbarians, darkness will take the place of light.

In the 1939-45 War the Russian-American Alliance with the collaboration of Britain flew over the ancient and beautiful city of Nürnberg and bombed it virtually off the face of the earth. It was a civic target, men, women and children perished in their thousands. After the war Wagner's grandson mounted a production of the opera on an almost bare stage devoid of the medieval city which had always formed the setting for the opera. People called it 'Die Meistersinger ohne Nürnberg'. The Mastersingers Without Nürnberg. This makes nonsense of Wagner's opera, and his whole philosophy. Indeed, his opera has triumphed and proved the reality, that the art has had the reality embedded in it, and the historical truth for that reason could not be destroyed. However much for political reasons people wanted to and did obliterate the city it arose again because it is embodied not in its bricks and mortar but in this glorious five hour song of joy for life and love and humanity, Germany's special gift to the world, and the core of our civilisation.

'I am counting on having depicted THE real nervecentre of German life,' wrote Wagner. He also wrote: 'No pathos, no ecstasy, but emotional depths, good humour; I like to think that there is hope on this foundation.' This is the unarguable and glorious foundation of his most loved achievement. In the end we are asked to accept that the freedom of Germany from foreign domination is fundamental to the continuance of that civilisation founded on its values. As in Lohengrin, he again warns of foreign dominance, this time not from the East but from the West. The work concludes in a vast confirmatory statement, the great C major close:

Ehrt eure deutschen Meister:	Honour your German
dann bannt ihr gute Geister!	Masters, Let them be your good spirits
Und gebt ihr ihrem Wirken Gunst,	Follow their works
zerging' in Dunst	then even if the Holy
das heil'ge röm'sche Reich,	Roman Empire dissolve in mist
uns bliebe gleich	for us would still remain
die heil'ge deutsche Kunst!	our Holy German Art!

On the 7th October, 1864, Wagner was officially

'commanded' to complete the Ring for Ludwig II. On the 24th October, 1867, he completed the score of the Meistersinger and sent the good news to the King and von Bülow signing himself 'Sachs'. Renewed and inspired by the completion of these two great works his mind again returned to the task of completing the Ring. On the 24th of June, 1868, while travelling he was suddenly possessed with the final triumphant theme of Siegfried. But on reaching Triebschen he was taken ill. By the summer he was considering an opera which would have as its theme the marriage of Luther. Once more he had turned to his concept of the couple as the human entity. Not until 1869, however, did he take up the task of composing the third act of Siegfried.

The end of Siegfried and the whole of the Götterdämmerung are enriched in texture and technique by the discoveries that came in the composition of Tristan and Meistersinger. The gain in musical power and expression is astonishing, but it only serves to underline the effectiveness and structural unification brought about by the motive system by which the whole work is sustained.

The long time span involved in creating the Ring necessarily implied that not only had the artist's means of expression become more effective and magisterial but also that his experience of life had changed. It is in the light of his changed material and political position that people judge the final parts of the Ring. Much has been made of the transition from revolutionary hero to reactionary master, subsidised by the mad and decadent monarch, implying that the composer having found that his bread was not only buttered by royal decree but honeyed, decided after all that the status quo was best. It must be pointed out that a great deal of the misconception of Wagner stems from the fact that the school, and for that matter University, textbook view, has been based on an outdated scholarship. A picture of Wagner formed by early opinion and prejudice is further weakened by the lack of necessary data. It was partly this lack of knowledge, and not just the 'old-fashioned' intellect, that made Wagner inaccessible in early writings, and as a result forced people into extreme partisanship or bitter opposition. There is no doubt that the Bayreuth clique after Wagner's death invited rational resistance, although in the end their loyalty opened a way to a broader critical assessment.

New scholarship has brushed aside these tedious tomes like Newman's and gone straight to original sources. The uncovering of the Red Book, the Brown Book and the Annals, the important contribution of the edited Journals of Cosima, the emergence of serious biographical research in the writing of Martin Gregor-Dellin and musical research in Curt von Westernhagen have opened a way to the new and more balanced as well as the appreciative, rather than adulatory at one extreme like Houston Chamberlain, or poisonous at the other like Adorno.

It can now be seen that Wagner basically remained the same radical he was at the beginning, even if he narrowed his concept of what was socially possible in the way of political transformation. We can now grasp that alongside his support from Ludwig there came the long awaited and deserved reputation and world wide fame that he quite rightly considered to be his due. Thus, in his last years, we see him, confirmed by an adulation and fame never before accorded a musician, and yet still enmeshed in struggle to present his works according to his vision. If anything the isolation and aloneness of his early years is repeated and experienced more profoundly at the end of his life. What Wagner gained was not patronage and fame, although without these he could never have completed his titanic life's work, but a home, a wife and children. The few romantic crushes at the end of his life never threatened the wonderful happiness he knew with Cosima and his children. No man has ever given his wife a more loving gift than Wagner gave to Cosima. On Christmas Day, also Cosima's Birthday, Wagner spirited into the hall of their house at Triebschen a small orchestra. Cosima awakened to the strains of the Siegfried Idyll which he had composed for her. Richter conducted it to the enchanted listeners who huddled on the stairs, among them the lonely figure of their guest, Friedrich Nietzsche.

He had early on written that what separated him from true revolutionaries was that their necessary historical task was to destroy the old order, and his role was to create. He was an artist. His vision was his contribution. What we can now see is that as a man he carried in himself both his remarkable and radical vision of a possible future alongside his quotidian view of how life was in his epoch, riddled as that was with contradictions, and caught as it was in the deep groundswell of long-term change, as Germany was forced into nation-hood and Empire in statist terms, very far from his visionary view of the German Volk, guardians of the deep tradition of western civilisation.

It is in the light of this dual situation that it is necessary to view Wagner's final controversial work. Not that this view will 'solve' the problems it raises but it will inform them significantly. For it seems that while his contribution to humanity was embodied in his great works, the Ring, Tristan and the Meistersinger, his contribution to his own life's understanding, and his act of making peace with existence and himself was embodied in this last, most intellectually alien and most musically profound drama, Parsifal.

With Parsifal we are taken right back to the world of Tannhäuser, where in an appropriately modern way, the original medieval author of the epic poem Parsifal figures as a character, Wolfram von Eschenbach. There, Wolfram is the exponent of pure love as opposed to the sensual love defended by Tannhäuser. The legend, even after receiving the usual Wagnerian pruning and telescoping and integrating at which he had already become an expert, is forbidding and remote material. It is the realm of the Waste Land, and the king with the dolorous wound, recalling Tristan, it is the secret terrain of a spiritual brotherhood and a pleasure garden which recalls the Venusberg. It has an innocent as its rescuing hero, recalling Siegfried. Its one startlingly original creation is the passionate Kundry, both demonic and spiritual, also longing for release. Into the strange doomed world of the two realms, that of the Grail people and that of Klingsor who was forbidden to join their ranks, comes Parsifal, the poor fool who in the end will experience compassion and save their world. It is a spiritual and psychic drama but without human conflict. The Grail does not celebrate the christian sacrament as a means to salvation, but rather puts forward the model of the compassionate and pure saint as the active transformer of life. It cannot be over-emphasised how alien and remote this world of the Grail is to us, much more so than the simple legends of his early music dramas. Yet if we have the courage and the stamina to enter it, the intensity of its expression utterly captures and enthrals.

The music of Parsifal is as directly engaging as its story is repellent. Of course, for us we are with this his last work, listening to the beginning of modern music, we have arrived at the present. Parsifal opened the path to the atonality and destructuring of music which followed in its wake.

As to the ideological content of the work, it is here that we encounter 'the Parsifal problem'. Here, inevitably the antagonist is Nietzsche, and given his importance to Wagnerian oeuvre and, later, Wagnerian identity, he cannot be ignored in this any more than he can be in philosophy simply because political populism has decided he is a threat. Having taken into account that necessary subjective and biographical realignment implied by the new research into the historical cause of Nietzsche's alienation from his master, it is nonetheless necessary to take into account that dimension of inescapable insight which accompanied him simply because he was who he was, a great philosopher, committed to authentic encounter. Thus, alienated from Wagner for whatever reasons, he had to somewhere, put his finger on the Achilles' heel of the Wagnerian view, or in a more appropriate metaphor, he had to point out, as Brünnhilde did to Hagen, the indefensible point on the back of the beloved 'Siegfried'. This was the classical price to be paid for betrayal. Wagner was his Siegfried hero, Wagner was, as Gregor-Dellin uncompromisingly puts it, the love of Nietzsche's life.

While so much of what he was to write about Wagner took on more and more this subjective element of strife rather than being informed with the usual lance-like thrusts of this great intellect, until for example, one is embarrassed to be told that Bizet's Carmen is to satisfy us in lieu of the Wagnerian world we are ordered to negate, it is when he touches on Parsifal that we experience the shock of recognition. What, in the end we may say is that it is precisely because the Wagnerian oeuvre is so saturated with the Nietzschean vision (or vice versa, or in mutuality) that when we come upon a work that enters into open negation of that view we cannot fail to experience the shock of recognition when it is pointed out to us.

The Nietzschean view is that Wagner had betrayed his titanic attempt to break through the Romantic 'barrier' and reach a new vision of human renewal, had succumbed to all of those elements which had most subjectively lured him in his early days, and that he had allowed his sexual guilt to inhibit him from confirming the fruit of sensual pleasure as spiritual knowledge, thus making a new 'religion' out of refusal, that is to say, out of asceticism, which in turn entailed a new lease of life to the very christian-jewish collaboration of ressentiment which Nietzsche had set himself to declare once and for all the enemy of life and the death of western civilisation.

That there is a small group of confused christians who look to Parsifal to uphold their bizarre religion of ritual homeopathic anthropophagism is not in itself a proof that Wagner's last work is 'christian', and Nietzsche's claim is much more serious than simply that the work rests on these antique and spurious foundations. What is interesting is that there exists a serious body of opinion which does not accept the Nietzschean critique, and, of course, their position has been strengthened considerably by the recent biographical uncoverings which have gone a long way to confirm that unease we have always felt about Nietzsche's highly subjective and ambiguous response to Wagner, his beloved master. Their case rests on the internal evidence that the work is a post-christian vision with a new 'redeemer' who saves without having to die a ritual and sacrificial death. The implications of their view, or perhaps their view simply is, that Parsifal is, in fact, a Nietzschean drama, after all, negating transcendence, speaking in purely human terms, as Wagner had always insisted he did. Nietzsche's 'Human, all too Human' is a fitting Wagnerian phrase, and the perfect motto of Wotan.

The case for a post-christian Parsifal rests on the text and the musical super-structure and so must be taken seriously. It is also being argued by a new generation of Wagnerians with more highly trained minds than either the earlier detractors or idolaters. If Parsifal is not simply presiding over a rare sectarian Communion then clearly something of great import is taking place in the last act. The most profound meditation on the matter has been exercised by Michael Tanner in his seminal text for new thinking on Wagner, 'The Total Work of Art'. He observes that Parsifal finds his meaning in 'entsündigte Natur', transfigured Nature, and quotes from the text the key words:

Ihn selbst am Kreuze kann (Natur) nicht erschauen:
da blickt sie zum erlösten Menschen auf.

'No more can (Nature) see Him Himself
on the Cross:
it looks up to redeemed mankind.'

The work ends with the uncompromising words:

Höchsten Heiles Wunder!	Miracle of highest salvation!
Erlösung dem Erlöser!	Redemption to the Redeemer!

If, as this view argues, redemption is a metaphor for self-knowledge, and self-realisation, then the procedure of the Brotherhood, following its new King's wisdom, is one of achieving self-acceptance imbued with understanding ('compassion') thus transforming the Grailists into a school for existential liberation. Again this view proposes nothing less than what we have already noted right at the beginning with Tannhäuser, and that is, that Wagner has taken the most recalcitrant legendary material, saturated with christian symbolism and deliberately subverted it to his own radical existential doctrines of salvation and liberation. He never ceased to be a theorist and a systematic thinker, but AS artist never with illusion that he was a philosopher. This was the very element that irresistibly attracted the psychologist Nietzsche, and inevitably bamboozled the abstract thinker, Schopenhauer. Wagner knew that in the end philosophical propositions embody themselves, privately or socially, and that manifested in art they would speak to the whole Volk and become instruments of transformation. The occident was steeped in a defunct christianism whose rituals survived their civic disbelief, and just as the town celebration of a christian festive saint's day in Meistersinger does not celebrate Saint Johannes but openly enthrones the city poet, Hans Sachs, so too in this final Wagnerian opus, Parsifal is not the Celebrant of a christian sect, but the celebrated, the liberated and liberating man. Now let us examine further the Nietzschean personal view of Parsifal.

Nietzsche had read the text of Parsifal when it was sent to him by Wagner. He heard the Parsifal Prelude in 1887. He never saw the completed work in the theatre. His famous or infamous accusation went as follows:

'At that time it was indeed high time TO SAY FAREWELL: and I immediately received a confirmation of the fact. Richard Wagner, seemingly the all-conquering, actually a decaying, despairing romantic, suddenly sank down helpless and shattered before the christian cross... Was there no German with eyes in his head, empathy in his conscience, for this dreadful spectacle? Was I the only one who suffered from it? Enough, this unexpected event illumined for me like a flash of lightning the place I had left – and likewise gave me those subsequent horrors that he feels who has passed through a terrible peril unawares. As I went on alone, I trembled; not long afterwards I was sick, more than sick, I was weary of the unending disappointment with everything we modern men have left to inspire us, of the energy, labour, hope, youth, love everywhere DISSIPATED; weary with disgust at the femininity and ill-bred rapturousness of this romanticism, weary of the whole idealist pack of lies and softening of conscience that had here once again carried off the victory over one of the bravest; weary, last but not least, with the bitterness of a suspicion – that after this disappointment, I was condemned to mistrust more profoundly, despise more profoundly, to be more profoundly alone than ever before. My TASK – where had it gone? What? Was it now not as if my task had withdrawn from me, as though I would for a long time to come cease to have any right to it? How was I going to be able to endure this GREATEST of privations? – I began by FORBIDDING myself, totally and on principle, all romantic music, that ambiguous, inflated, oppressive art that deprives the spirit of its severity and cheerfulness and lets rampant every kind of vague longing and greedy spongy desire. 'CAVE MUSICAM' is to this day my advice to all who are man enough to insist on cleanliness in things of the spirit; such music unnerves, softens, feminises, its 'eternal womanly' draws US – downwards!...'[23]

The whole long Preface to Part Two of 'Human all too Human' written at Oberangadin in 1886 from which this is excerpted reveals not so much an acute critical and insighted faculty at work but rather a man in the throes of a profound personal crisis, and one involving deep suffering. Throughout this important book Nietzsche returns again and again to the subject of Wagner always with that uncomfortable mixture of massive respect coupled with bitter accusation and sarcasm. The work ends with a strange duologue between two characters whom he names the Shadow and the Wanderer. In the light of the importance of Wagner to him, which he has frankly confessed at the beginning of the work, perhaps we should look at this strange Beckett-like encounter in the knowledge that he was the 'shadow' of Wagner in the heady days of his discipleship, and that Wagner was inescapably identified with the character of Wotan in his creative role. Wotan's name incognito was the

Wanderer, he who as Light-Alberich saw his opponent as his shadow, Black-Alberich. Here are a few exchanges from the close of the book:

The Shadow: ... For – admit it – you have hitherto been only too happy to slander us.

The Wanderer: Slander? But why have you never defended yourself? You were close enough to our ear, after all.

———————

The Shadow: It is often with sorrow that I have deserted you: it seems to me, who am greedy for knowledge, that much that is dark still adheres to man because I cannot always be with him. If the reward were a perfect knowledge of man I might even agree to be your slave.

———————

The Wanderer: Oh, is it time for us to part? And I had to end by hurting you; I saw it, you grew darker as I did it.

The Shadow: I blushed, in the colour in which I am able to blush. It occurred to me that I have often lain at your feet like a dog, and that you then –

The Wanderer: And could I not, in all haste, do something to please you? Is there nothing you want?

The Shadow: Nothing, except perhaps that which the philosophical 'dog' desired of the great Alexander: that you should move a little out of the sunlight, I am feeling too cold.'[24]

Gregor-Dellin in his Wagner biography outlines the story of how Dr. Otto Eiser, founder of the Frankfurt Wagner Society and author of a serious study on the Ring met up with Nietzsche and later became his doctor. Wagner's concern for his friend's welfare led to an over-solicitous and over-intimate exchange between himself and the doctor. Wagner was morally incorrect, but the doctor professionally inexcusable. In any event, Wagner conveyed to the doctor his concern that the reason for Nietzsche's decline was a result of the practice of masturbation. A series of exchanges passed between the composer and the doctor on the subject heavily weighted by the contemporary view on the subject. The outcome of this breach of respect for Nietzsche, inevitably, was that someone leaked the news to the philosopher, assuring an inevitable break. Gregor-Dellin points out Nietz-sche's later reference to the incident which he indicated with the veiled observation: '... But there is something between us like a mortal insult...'[25] He then went on to refer openly to the incident of the letters while blurring the nature of the issue.

What is important to us in all this is the standing of Parsifal and the true character of the Nietzsche/Wagner relationship. After hearing the Prelude he was to write:

> 'Has Wagner ever done anything better?... there occurs in the very depth of this music a sublime and extraordinary feeling, a living experience and an event of the soul which does great honour to Wagner, a synthesis of states which many people, including our 'superior' intellectuals, will regard as incompatible: an awful severity of judgment 'from on high' which issues from an intimate understanding of the soul and sees through the soul, piercing it as with knives – and hand in hand with this goes a compassion for what has been perceived and judged. Only Dante is comparable, nobody else.'[26]

The listeners in the end must judge for themselves.

Here, embedded in this medievalism, saturated with this tremendous new kind of music, shimmering and changing in texture, tonality fading and melting in inexplicable shifts of key and changes of harmony, is to be found Wagner's most difficult and serious statement about the human self, in a vision which totally affirms the worthwhileness of the human venture and all its pain. If the human situation as a social bonding experience of brotherhood and joy is the theme of the Meistersinger then the human experience as isolation and self-confrontation and triumphing over suffering is the theme of Parsifal. The compassion is not passivity but re-generation. The offer is not the annihilation of the Ring with its necessarily disturbing ambiguity, but rather a great peace. It is – whatever we decide about it – one of the summits of human creativity.

It is almost impossible to overestimate the importance of Wagner for Nietzsche. How linked they are is more and more apparent. And just as Nietzsche, after the break, had to appropriate into himself the Wagnerian Other when thinking ideologically, and pay ludicrous homage to Bizet in lieu of the Master in his musical world, so Wagner had to look to other models to replace the ongoing dialogue which before had so enriched them both. As for Nietzsche's frank and bitter reference to the 'eternal womanly' which he claimed so ominously dragged him downwards, reversing Goethe's claim, we must return to that theme later. Wagner, on the other hand, knew exactly what his view of woman was. Established on a wide and complex set of female relationships, both erotic and platonic, Wagner had constructed a radical and liberating doctrine of women and their role in the new society. As we have already noted, his view of women evolved, as indeed did his view of men. With Parsifal completed, Wagner, exhausted in his Venice palazzo, allowed his thoughts to turn again to the vital importance of the new woman in his vision of the future. He had begun an essay entitled, 'Über das Weibliche im Menschlichen', 'On Feminism in Humanism'. It was while engaged in its text, he had started it two days before his death, that the pen slipped from his fingers and his final communication was interrupted. To the end he had meditated his deepest themes, and up until his last days he had studied and read aloud from the world's great masterworks, listened at the piano to his beloved Beethoven, and those other composers whose work he so enjoyed, Bach, Mozart, and his friend and father-in-law, Liszt. His life had been deeply meditated and studied, alongside his turbulent erotic adventures and his even more tempestuous political forays, there had been always that amazing capacity to withdraw to his desk and compose music. In the end when we talk of Wagner we are talking of a musician, whatever we may say and deduce about his dramatic genius and his intellectual virility it is as composer that we confront both his greatness and his universality. He silences his critics by his sound. That he had taken music into a new realm where it had never been before is another story, and yet it is that story which is so intriguing. What did he possess that no other composer did, and which has this unique effect on us, and in truth is the cause of all the controversy?

As usual Nietzsche speaks the key phrase: 'He (Wagner) has immeasurably increased the speaking power of music.'[27] Now he did not mean the power of music when it is utilising the spoken word, that is, in the musical phrasing of his dramatic dialogues. He meant that Wagner had increased the power of music TO SPEAK.

We have to ask: how can we talk of music 'speaking'? In what sense can it speak, and if it can, what can it speak? It seems implicit in Nietzsche's phrase that he already considered music possessed the capacity of 'speech', what he discerned with Wagner was an extension of this capacity, therefore an ability to bring music to the point where it could handle new – what? Matters? New themes? Ideas, feelings?

Two things must be noted chez Wagner, one is his radical development of existing modes and manners of expression, the other is his moving the whole event of musical expression onto a completely new, qualitatively new level of coherence and capacity. We can discern quite without difficulty a development from early baroque string quartets through the fluency and seriousness of Haydn's to the gravely meditated last quartets of Beethoven. Equally, we can see the enormous gain in sophistication of feeling and subject-matter from Gluck's Orpheo through Mozart's Don Giovanni up to the mature political reflection of Beethoven's Fidelio. Yet between all these and the four great works that are the Wagner achievement there is a hiatus. It is not that one is in the game of saying this work of art is better than that, or of aligning oneself with a composer to suit one's temperament. We will not be able to get at the depths of the Nietzschean observation unless we can recognise what Wagner introduced with his late, and utterly unpredicted transformation of the opera form into what he was to rename music-drama, and which he was to prepare an unsuspecting, and in retrospect a remarkably receptive, public to receive through a series of difficult, and at times seemingly deliberately obtuse, theoretical works which in themselves introduced a whole series of new aesthetic categories of forbidding erudition and original terminology.

In 1928 Richard Strauss wrote in a letter: 'I happen to be reading Richard Wagner's Oper und Drama once again, a splendid book as relevant today as it was eighty years ago and still every bit as uncomprehended and unknown.'[28] There is no doubt that in these difficult texts Wagner was preparing the ground for his own new creations which would be the demonstrations of his arguments. So astonishing was his success that half way through his great creative period he announced that he had gone beyond his own theories. In dealing with Wagner's theories of the basis of speech and music we must hold two elements in critical isolation; first, the theory in itself, as valid and useful or not, and second, how that theory translated itself into a successful model of the evolution implied.

The most intriguing aspect of the Wagnerian view which is not naive simply because it is described in a convoluted language – is that his view of language and music directly forms the basis of his political ideology. According to Wagner the basis of human language is tone-speech, that is variant vowels over a range of pitch. This is what he portrays as primal speech in the wonderful song of the Rhine Daughters which was the expression of emotions. The interruptive effect of consonantal sounds allowed identification of objects until words emerged. From there speech moved its emotional base to an ideational base. The emergence of syntax implied as it were the repression of the underlying music in speech. Assonance of consonants, like in the ancient stabreim with its alliterative inner structure, kept the door open to feeling. As speech moved away from its inner melodic capacity to a broader and more discursive faculty which ended in 'the grey morass of prose',[29] music extracted itself from the feeling foundations of primal tone-speech and became expressed first in song and lyric and then in instrumental form. 'Pure' music was the balancing factor in the arrival at cold syntactical speech. In the end we have two languages: grammar based speech and harmonic speech, each with its own notation.

Wagner makes a parallel analysis of the growth of drama. He examines the roots of drama in the Greeks, the Italian folk theatre, and the resultant 'modern' expression of Shakespeare on the one hand and Racine on the other, with German theatre somewhere in the middle. He notes the falling away of the musical and lyrical dimension of drama and its chorus, until we arrive at the didactic spoken play. Do not forget that as Wagner was making his works of synthesis, Ibsen, as master dramatist was leaning towards a more lyrical theatre – ending in duologues very similar to those profound encounters that set the Wagner oeuvre apart from all opera but very near late Ibsen. But the genius of Wagner's thinking, and his music-dramas are its fruit, lies in his connecting the decay of the fullest artistic expression – the drama – with the rise of the structuralist state; Wagner sees the rise of the state as we know it not as an evolution and progress for man but as a disastrous imprisoning of man which will end in his total destruction unless itself destroyed. He claimed that primal drama projected an image of man in his freedom and thus preserved the Volk, while Romance projected the passive functionary of the state, spiritually dead and obedient. So at the heart of the Wagnerian weltanschauung is an open declaration of war on Romanticism. That he attacked it from within makes all the more remarkable both his own evolution and his triumph as a creative genius.

The fragmentation and destruction of life quality in structural statism would end, declared Wagner, with the annihilation of man. The metaphysical encasement which man experienced as a being in the world – coming out of nothing and returning into the void, yet in his brief spell finding himself the lord of life – gave man his glory and led him to extract from his suffering the nectar of human love. The negation of the basic biological condition of man through thought-processes, and through the pursuit of material goals, resulted in the replacement of life confrontation with the futile pursuit of politics, particularly utopian politics, which delay any result of his struggle. Thus political man, through being political was doomed to a life of meaninglessness and sterility. This meant that the state, the structuralist edifice, supposedly constructed for the protection and preservation of man resulted in his total spiritual annihilation, indeed, in the end of man as such.

Wagner held that the way out of the dilemma was the exploration – not of new political concepts which would only further entrap man – of the most ancient human myths, Volk myths, for each people had their mythic inheritance to show them their root condition. The political state thrives on crime and vice for they permit it to strengthen its hold over the good citizens under the pretext of prevention – in that sense terrorism could be taken as the sign of ultimate state tyranny and success. The state, wielding as it does absolute power and control is in fact itself capricious, goalless, and can only offer the people carnival and superficial play. The key to free individuals is the opposite, that inwardly they possess an inner drive of necessity. Wagner observes that since the free man no longer exists, only man as created by the state, that is conditioned by frivolity and lack of goal, nowhere recognising inner necessity, which implies existential knowledge of oncoming death and its acceptance, it becomes the duty of the poet to imagine the free man, being as we have said unable to portray him as a historical reality. Wagner realises that the 'idea' of the free man will not penetrate state conditioning, for the speech forms have been subverted in the political process so that man cannot 'hear' and only responds to abstract ideas which will alter nothing. What Wagner calls 'abstract and conditioned word speech' is ineffective in the desired awakening of men. As he puts it: 'The return from understanding to feeling will be the march of the drama of the future, in so far as we shall advance from the THOUGHT-OUT individuality to the genuine one.'[30] Wagner's solution to the dilemma is to present again to man his true identity in a mythic construction which will speak to us directly imbuing the intellectual response with deep and direct feeling, restoring the 'purely-human' dimension of man which has been anaesthetised by dead syntax. The emergence of the free, because self-determined individual, will imply the inevitable down fall of the structuralist (or constitutional) state. It is now possible to see that the Wagnerian concept is very far from the naive back-to-nature views of Rousseau and others. Wagner certainly insists that man is a natural animal and has been cut off from his natural identity, but he nowhere imagines that man has to 'get back to nature' to be happy. Siegfried is compelled by his freedom to go down the Rhine to confront political man. Parsifal's enthronement implies that the Grail-ists must get out into the world. Only a succumbing to the impulse to plunge into nature itself in the erotic drive would lead to disaster, one deliciously desired by the natural man, and his perpetual but necessary risk, (the Tristan syndrome).

Here, in these concepts, the spirit of Wagner can be seen as being very close to the spirit of Beethoven. It is interesting to note that our modern understanding of Beethoven was almost completely negotiated to us by Wagner, from a musical point of view. Yet Beethoven as radical thinker was obscured from us by the cheap 'Romantic' concepts put forward by the obedient statist apologist, the academics and critics. So, to take the next step in our understanding of what happened to musical expression through Wagner's contribution we must first get some idea of how Wagner saw Beethoven's prior evolutionary jump in its qualitative trans-formation.

According to Wagner's analysis, Beethoven, the first modern musician found himself trapped in the world created by the structuralist state and sought passionately to produce out of the prison of mechanical life the image of man, the original free being. Over and against mechanisation and slavery stood melody, and that 'spoke' man. Man was in reality 'none other than Melody, that is the moment of most definite, most convincing utterance of music's actual living organism.'[31] But it was not until the point where Beethoven reached his Ninth Symphony that the explosion occurred. 'Every musical organism is by its nature feminine, it is a pregnant and not a seminal force. The seminal force lies outside it. And without fecundation by this force it cannot bear.'[32] With the seminal force of Schiller the genius of Beethoven found its expression, firstly it merely expressed itself alongside the poet providing a tune, but then the composer took the words and fused the two languages into one which could express all that the composer had desired to say but without the words of Schiller could not.

Yet even that might just seem like a licence for the kind of activity Wagner indulged in himself playing both Schiller and Beethoven. However Wagner does not leave the matter there and his case does not rest on his own idiosyncratic reading of the Ninth. He then goes further, and here he is also thinking, as he often did, of the Quartets. 'The characteristic of the great compositions of Beethoven is that they are actual poems: that in them it is sought to bring a real subject to representation.' Wagner insists at great length that this is the case and that the expert in pure music cannot possibly arrive at Beethoven's intention or respond to his work in a way that will permit him to grasp its meaning.

In 'Opera and Drama', the essay spoken of so emphatically by Richard Strauss, it says: 'The history of instrumental music, from the moment when the longing first manifest, is the history of an artistic error; yet one that ended, not in the demonstration of an impotence of music, like that of the operatic genre, but with the revelation of a boundless inner power. The error of Beethoven was that of Columbus, who merely meant to seek out a new way to the old known land of India, and discovered a new land instead. For us, too, here there has been unveiled the inexhaustible power of music, through Beethoven's all powerful error. Through his undaunted struggle to reach the artistically Necessary within an artistically Impossible, is shown us music's unhemmed faculty of accomplishing every thinkable task, if only she is content to stay what she really is – an art of EXPRESSION.'[33]

At first Beethoven simply wrote within the

spirit of his musical epoch... 'But from the time when, in concord with the moving sorrows of his life, there awoke in the artist a longing for distinct expression of specific, characteristically individual emotions – as though to bare himself to the intelligent sympathy of his fellow men – and this longing grew into an ever more compulsive force; from the time when he began to care less and less about merely making music, about expressing himself agreeably, enthrallingly or inspiritingly in general, within that music; and instead was driven by the necessity of his inner being to employ his art in bringing to sure and graspable expression a definite content that absorbed his thought and feeling – there began the agony of this troubled and restless artist. Those powerful outbursts and the half-sorrowful, half-blissful stammerings of a Pythian inspiration, could only give the impression of a genius struck by madness to the curious listener who did not understand him simply because the inspired man could not possibly make himself intelligible to such a one.' They could not understand him because they were not 'listening' to Beethoven's expression but were listening to a music that they expected to delight them and distract them. Had they opened themselves to what he had done to music they would have grasped it directly. Talking of the second half of Beethoven's life, Wagner continues: 'The greater portion of Beethoven's works of this period must be regarded as instinctive attempts to frame a speech to voice his longing.'[34]

This was the inheritance of Wagner – a fully forged musical syntax that could express a human condition and thus itself convey 'idea'. If this were the claim of a critic or a musicologist embedded in theories of music it might be dismissed, but it simply cannot when it is the viewpoint of a composer who then goes on to build on this theoretical foundation and create an entirely new kind of aesthetic experience.

What Wagner did was to take this forged musical syntax, wed it to verbal syntax in a fusion which was then projected alive in a dramatic context before the public, and that drama was itself a retelling of mythic material dredged up from the remote past of that Volk, thus connecting them at the deepest possible psychological level and short-circuiting the subversive attempt of the structuralist state to isolate the people from their own natural roots and identity, for reconnected to their true nature they would destroy the state which tyrannised them.

While Wagner, like Ibn Rushd, maintained a sentimental attachment to the idea of a valuable hereditary monarch who would represent the

Republic, his conviction remained – as did the medieval philosopher's and Beethoven's – wedded to the platonic concept of the Republic. The function of this new fusion of music and poetry embedded in the dramatic confrontation between the myth and its Volk was not to be cathartic, purging the citizens and then sending them dutifully back home, nor for that matter was it 'revolutionary art' designed to drive you to the barricades or convince you of a propagandist view of life like the barren theatre of Brecht. Rather, it was meant to plunge you into the profound streaming of your own consciousness which would in turn touch its source in the mythic explanation of the basic forces at play in the world. Nothing could be further from this view than the psycho-analytic one which reduces all experience to the waste matter of the repressed Unconscious be it personal or cosmic. The effect of this bathing in the deepest energy sources of existence would restore the public to life refreshed and invigorated, the final result would be one of revitalisation and conviction in man's capacity for transformation. As the inheritor of this musical syntax he was also the follower of the creator of Fidelio and the Ninth, and so was well aware that the immediate result of this great synthesis would be to point to the liberation that had to come from the new and authentic psyche. While he saw this as essentially a model for the future and always insisted that his public was a public of the future, yet its great significance is that this 'total work of art' serves both to connect us to our past and let us draw meaning from it as well as to be invigorated and not defeated by the chaos of the present. Since this new creation that Wagner proposed to his society nevertheless was dependent on this musical evolution it is important to look more at just what it was that Wagner did in creating this music-text-myth embedded in dramatic conflict projected by men and women and thus also employing the plastic expression of human bodies.

The symphonic frame of a Wagner work is the narrative form of the drama which it presents. Into that casing is poured the mix of aesthetic elements, music, text, and theatrical plasticity that make up the full impact of the final experience. The overture is already a thing of the past. Preludes prepare the public for the mood and content of the drama to come. Far from being anthological in its musical substance, it is an introductory orientation of the listener's psyche to open them up for the journey that lies ahead. Of course the great Preludes stand alone as orchestral works, but their meaning and impact is based on that preparatory atmosphere which creates in the listener an anticipatory tension that is only relieved by plunging into the action itself. Thus, before the curtain is up we are considering a psychological state, empathy, and ambience.

It is now wisely agreed that the use of the leading-motive method of identifying key phrases by name is disastrous to the over-all complexity and sophistication of the Wagnerian technique. Not only are many of these brief phrases disastrously ill-named, and thus pervert the author's original vision, but also they reduce to a simplistic trick what is in actuality an enormously complex system. So complex is it, we can safely say it has never been fully charted, and perhaps could not be definitively. At best we would finish with several basic maps of the thematic so called motives. Deryck Cooke in his uncompromising rejection of naming leading-motives points out Wagner's 'phenomenal power of compressing into a few bars the most profound emotional and psychological experience, which makes conceptual thematic labels quite pointless.'

This sub-structure of basic simple thematic phrases exists and some adhere to characters and objects, others emerge at crucial moments of particular emotional response and embody particular feelings and sometimes these move out into wider melodic phrases and at other times melodic expression appears and does not re-appear. This flow of music is given its particular quality by the use of harmony and the increasingly intricate web of tonality that is used, a tonality that as the method becomes more and more expert begins itself to break up and vanish under the impact of the chromatic richness of expression. In the end the Wagnerian sound has become, in his own words 'the one great melody of the forest'.

The flow of changes caused by these elements work together, on the one hand the firmly identifiable phrases, the ill-named motives, and on the other the sonority of the Wagnerian orchestration made fluid and thick with interweaving changes in motive alongside abrupt changes in rhythm and key – so much of the music of Wagner if lifted out of context and presented as a chunk of sound would not be identified as his but would seem to be the product of a contemporary composer so at home is he with sudden shifts of key, dissonance, and unfinished harmonies. This musical flow is like the flow of meridians in the chinese acupuncture system, identifiable only by the surfacing of individual points, the musical phrases connecting to persons, key objects and emotions.

The effect of the sonority, the famous Wagner 'sound', is related to a connected effect, and actually dominated by it. The textual idea dictates the forward movement of the sound. Here, the poetry pinpoints the emotion and the psyche and the reason for the immediate anguish or delight. Wagner uses narration of past events with an undisputed expertise, like Aeschylus, his master and model. So adept was he at portraying in his music the mental condition of the character that unsurprisingly he took the opportunity to show off to us how effective he was at it with his game, his lethal game, played by Siegfried on Mime, once the former has learned to interpret the real thoughts behind the words. The Forest Bird is a perfect metaphor for the Wagnerian process. Just as the bird reveals the true emotions to Siegfried, so Wagner, using his 'infinite melody' reveals to us the tremendous depths of human experience that lies hidden in the hearts. Wagner 'speaks' using the text, but reaches way beyond the text – in Tristan the text becomes a kind of free-association of unthought words – through the musical expression.

It is now that we see the complexity of what has been achieved for the text, sometimes glowingly poetic as in Meistersinger, sometimes psychologically apposite, sometimes banal, but always appropriate, remains only the speech of the event itself. Thus, to the connected effect of the textual idea has to be added the dramatic narrative, conflict and resolution. Many times a character is alone in silence and the music broods over them revealing to us in the most particular and definitive way what their condition is both emotionally and existentially. Part of the shattering impact of Siegfried's majestic Trauermarsch is that it accompanies the raising up of the dead hero who has just died so sublimely before our eyes with a nobility which has wiped out for us all our uncomfortable uncertainty about his instinctive behaviour previously. So we face death with those mixed emotions that are so human while at the same time experience another emotion that accompanies the act of bearing a dead body from a place.

One final but important element existed in the new system. Wagner himself named it the art of transition. He explained it lucidly to Mathilde Wessendonck. 'I now realise that the special fabric of my music (always, of course, most precisely related to the poetic conception), which my friends now regard as so new and so important, owes its construction above all to the highly sensitive feeling which directs me to interlink and inter-relate every element of transition between the most extreme moods. I should now like to call my deepest and most subtle art the art of transition, for the whole fabric of my art is built up on such transitions: sharp and sudden changes I have come to dislike; they are often unavoidable and necessary, but even then they may not occur unless the atmosphere has been so carefully prepared for the sudden change that it seems inevitable.' He goes on to explain the example of such a transition in the second act of Tristan. 'Now there you have the secret of my musical form, of which I am bold enough to assert that such a degree of consistency and clarity in a structure which embraces every detail has never before even been dreamed of. If you only knew to what extent that guiding principle has led me to musical ideas here – of rhythm, harmonic and melodic development – such as I could never hit on before, you would realise that even in the most specialised branches of art nothing worthwhile can be created unless it derives from such great principle motives. Well! That is art! But with me this art is very much related to life.'[35] With this final unexpected concept we have completed our description of the Wagner method.

In this description we have isolated the original musical effect and the connected textual idea wedded as it is to the dramatic and dynamic moment with its prior narrative force impinging on that present – and all this results in a total effect which is the Wagnerian experience. For all the supercilious rejection of the theoretical concept of the total-art-work, nevertheless, that is just what has been created. All this is the product of one intellect. It was this quite new complexity and quite ancient synthesis which Wagner brought to life for an astonished world which must be forgiven for having deified him for a time and in Queen Victoria's flat little phrase having gone 'quite crazy about him'.

The four masterworks are meant to go together, in a sense, to be one great statement on life. At one point to underline this Wagner wanted Parsifal to appear in Tristan as part of his earlier wanderings before his final liberating encounter in the forest, thus he would have gone from the forest of death to the forest of life, but in his wisdom he resisted the literalisation of his unified concept. Wagner, the revolutionary slowly evolved into an artist who meditated on the theme of transformation. He saw that the social change which superior men desired for the world, could only come about when man was himself liberated from the programming of the absolute state. He recognised that the problem was not one of structure, for in his time the communists had stolen, as had the 'democrats and constitutionalists' the name of that revolution which he and his companions longed for, as did Beethoven. In its name they were prepared simply to offer another tyrannical structure. What was required was a new man. This was the ultimate concern of Wagner and it is this theme that flows through all his works. Wagner had been the friend of Bakunin. It was Bakunin who split with Marx on the very issue of whether the revolution meant to conquer the state for new forces or dismantle it. Bakunin lost. The struggle passed from politics to art. Wagner, the radical, had to retreat into an uneasy and lonely subsidised existence, supported by the very decadence he loathed. Yet as an artist he would never betray his beliefs, as courageous in his creativity as Bakunin at the barricades. In 'Was nützt diese Erkenntnis?' Wagner declared himself committed to the struggle for the new man: 'We believe in the possibility of this regeneration and dedicate ourselves to its fulfilment in every respect.'[36]

The Ring is his great political testament. It is his narration of the cycle of political forces and their working out from beginning to end. In it he identifies both inward necessity and outer inescapability, not Fate but its politicisation, that men cannot stop themselves from following drives which dominate their actions up to the point that they do not know themselves. Siegfried's tragedy is that he finds out too late, Brünnhilde's victory is that she finds out just in time. This is what gives release from the curse of the Ring, and we will have to examine this in great detail. It is the Ring which raises as one of its central themes what lies beyond man as a hope for the world, the coming man, here only imagined, in order that men can one day realise the vision as a reality.

Tristan is his study of the erotic consciousness. It is neither meant to be a deliberate cathartic lesson – look, aren't you glad it wasn't you? – nor a lavish indulgence in absolute self-destruction through obsessional lust as his bitter critics imply, telling us more about them than about Wagner whose psyche has been scrutinised thoroughly. Tristan is a glorious celebration of the erotic consciousness in its fullness, which, utterly expressed must result in mutual annihilation. The composer reveals to us that the underlying 'opposites' of nature, man and woman, while mutually attracted to absolute union, take their life from the dividing line. The day/night symbolism of the astonishing text make clear that man/woman is one entity thus divided. It is from this that he can make his claim that the human being is in fact not the man, nor even the woman as modernists want to claim – but rather, the couple.

Meistersinger is the work which celebrates ordinary social life. It is not a strange aberration into normality from the fevered brain of a sick genius, it is at the core of Wagner's humanity, Germanness and universal spirit. It is his confirmation of faith in the human project and living with others, it is tolerant, generous and forgiving and full of mature resignation about the loneliness of life.

Parsifal, his most difficult and inaccessible work, is his study of the inner consciousness, as Meistersinger celebrates the civic one. The one honours the Volk, the other the man. Parsifal's coming to consciousness is the deep theme of this last work. Parsifal is another step towards the creation by man of the new man. Siegfried died in the web of politics, despite his greatness and because of it, for he could not compromise his freedom. Parsifal breaks free of his own condition by recognising it. He becomes self aware, not merely innocent. Man has taken a step. Then was not Wagner, like his great friend and loving disciple, Nietzsche, working for the same end – the liberation of the species by the bridge to the Overman? 'As for the real Wagner,' wrote Nietzsche, 'I myself will be to a great extent his heir.' Despite the more and more turbulent attacks on his former master it was in the end to be as he said, beyond the stirred dust of controversy. Nietzsche was Wagner's heir, carrying on a discourse which they together had initiated on those long summer walks by the lake at Triebschen and in the salon of Wahnfried.

3

DER RING DES NIBELUNGEN

DAS RHEINGOLD

Das Rheingold is the Preliminary Drama to the trilogy of the Ring. The myth starts and ends by the River Rhine. As the work opens we are at the bottom of the great river – at its end the Rhine will overflow its banks reclaiming the ring of power, but then we will look beyond its waters as Walhalla and the gods are consumed in flames and the whole life cycle comes to an end which had begun, as we entered the world of the Ring, to the vast swelling 136 bar E flat major chordal sequence that declared the beginning of a world in the depths of the sea.

With the opening of the first music-drama we are plunged not only into the murky waters of the river of life but into immediate confrontation with the central drama of the myth. The first scene is about a man being refused love and then refusing it. In Wagner's world it is the primal crime, and its working out and resolution is nothing less than history itself. What could be further from a Jungian, or indeed Freudian, point of view?

The negation of love in giving it and taking it is the life current that runs alongside the affirm-ation of political power making up the electrical current of tragedy which activates the whole cycle. Before the end, Fricka, denied Wotan's love will have doomed Siegmund to death, Wotan will deny his love for Brünnhilde and strip her of immort-ality, Siegfried, drugged into forgetfulness will deny Brünnhilde and in turn be destroyed. Only at the end will Brünnhilde resolve the conflict between love and power by 'crossing the wires' – rejecting power through her return of the Ring, and confirm love by willing her own end as her father had done, in turn confirming him: 'Ruhe, ruhe, du Gott.'

But before the protagonists can lock into their inexorable destinies the initial crime has to take place and it is this enthralling encounter that opens the cycle. On the one hand are the Daughters of the Rhine and on the other the Nibelung dwarf,

Alberich. The Rhine Daughters play together, their exchanges a meaningless yet ravishing swirl of song:

'Wagalaweia!
Wallala weiala weia!'

Alberich, ugly, with long locks of hair and bristling beard, is, to the Rhine Daughters simply a figure of fun. They tease him innocently, playing and flirting, unaware that they are rousing in the dwarf a violent hatred and ressentiment born out of his rejected advances. Their erotic game has reduced him to speechless rage when sunlight falls on the gold of the river. In his sexual anguish Alberich has cried out:

Wie in den Gliedern	Passionate fevers,
brünstige Glut	fervid desires,
mir brennt und glüht!	have set me on fire!
Wut und Minne	Rage and longing,
wild und mächtig	wild and frantic,
wühlt mir den Mut auf!	drive me to madness!

He falls, 'breathless and foaming with rage' at the moment when the illumined gold captures his attention. It seems that as the drama proceeds we find that the protagonists encounter their will to power inescapably intertwined with their fierce erotic energy. That is why Hagen, Alberich's son is so much more malevolent than his father, his identity being embedded solely in the envy of, and will to destroy, Siegfried. But with the appearance of the gold a new dimension of existence confronts the Nibelung dwarf. The unfulfilled erotic need is diverted to the gold. Soon it will be diverted to its essence, access to power itself.

The vision of the gold and its salutation by the Rhine Daughters is one of those moments that Wagner's mastery of orchestration could produce with such ease and originality. As the Rhinegold motive declares itself and the orchestra dazzles us by its streaming sound the Rhine Daughters greet the gold, exquisitely celebrating the sun's rays falling on the precious metal. Finally, the moment climaxes in their exultant cries of 'Rheingold! Rheingold!' It is a music we will hear again and again throughout the epic, each time more poignant and anguished, until finally it is part of the intricate, shuddering relief which announces that the Ring has at last been restored to its primal innocence in the depths of the great river.

Perhaps it will help our deeper contemplation of the myth if we know now, in advance of the tragedy, that the Ring which we will shortly have news of for the first time in this opening scene, is passed from one protagonist to another during the action. It is longed for, exulted in, guarded over and killed for, it passes from hand to hand, and while it destroys each person who takes it as theirs, it is never truly possessed, for in all the long disastrous story it will not once be used or serve its owner. Tarnhelm, spear and sword will serve their owners, draughts of forgetfulness and dragon's blood will change the destinies of men and women, but the Ring itself remains utterly passive, potential, and disastrous.

On first seeing the Rhinegold Alberich asks precisely about its usefulness. What is the gold 'for'? Wellgunde explains the power of the Ring.

Der Welt Erbe	The world's wealth can
gewänne zu eigen,	be won by a man who,
wer aus dem Rheingold	seizing the Rhinegold
schüfe den Ring,	fashions a ring:
der masslose Macht ihm	that ring makes him lord
verlieh'	of the world.

The next crucial revelation is that to master the gold it is necessary to pronounce a curse on love. Before the Ring can be forged – love must be renounced. The Rhine Daughters are confident that no man can live without love and that the gold is safe. Alberich's conviction that cunning can replace love as a passion decides him and he declares his fateful renunciation of love. The Nibelung dwarf has stolen the gold and plunged with it into the depths, but soon his action will reverberate above the clouds.

On the mountain heights towers the 'castle with gleaming battlements' newly completed, and below in the valley rolls the River Rhine, now bereft of its treasure. The castle, of course, is Walhalla, built as a home for the gods and the resurrected warriors of human battles. The pagan terminology should not put off the modern intellect, least of all the monotheist. There is no idea of the gods being 'god' in the metaphysical sense implying Being. Wotan defines their position in creation as spirits of light. They are the most evolved race of creatures in the saga. As ruler of the world, Wotan represents man in his present stage of consciousness. Writing to Röckel, Wagner explained: 'He resembles us to a hair. He is the sum of the intelligence of the present, whereas Siegfried is the man of the future whom we wish for and will to arrive, and yet cannot create – who must create himself by means of our annihilation.'[37]

It is highly significant, and crucial to the narrative, that Fricka, Wotan's wife, should be the goddess of marriage and its protector. Fricka, in this sense, is to contemporary women what Wotan is to modern men. They have, in short, the perfect bourgeois marriage. They have prestige without love. He has built for her a glorious castle in the sky only to increase her discontent. Fricka's arguments against Wotan, her husband, are irrefutable. That is not what matters – between them there flickers not a gleam of compassion, only a vanishing hope that by improving their material and political position things might get better. Fricka, too, is the victim of the failure of the monogamous system. Her husband has been serially unfaithful to her, siring a series of remarkable daughters, the Walküre, from his own race, and later, as he is driven more desperately, twins from a mortal woman. Fricka is enormously sympathetic, and her authority and disdain in their marital squabbles is utterly devoid of the slightest hint of misogynism on the author's part. The complexity of the characters in the Ring will reveal themselves to us, and not least by the narrative but the growingly coherent commentary of the musical language which describes their inner condition.

Walhalla is completed, but Fricka is only concerned about the cost. Wotan has commissioned the palace from the race of giants, and contracted Fafner and Fasolt to build it on condition that on its completion he would pay them by rewarding them the beautiful Freia, goddess of love and youth. It is by eating her apples that the gods retain their youth. Wotan in his ambition has put aside the problem, hoping, as he explains that it would all be solved by Loge, the god of fire. Walhalla is of enormous importance to Wotan. It represents not only power but evolution. Here he will receive the dead heroes from among the humans, thus setting up a new dimension in their situation below, breeding a new race who will aspire to the highest ideals of manhood. He is building a bridge to the Overman.

Mannes Ehre,	Manhood's honour,
ewige macht	unending power,
ragen zu endlosem Ruhm!	rise now to endless renown!

Wotan rules by his Spear on which are engraved the runes which outline the basic laws of the world. He has made them but he must abide by them. The Spear, basis of his authority, he cut from the 'tree of life' an act in itself devastating in its results. Man's (the gods') rule over the earth is in itself a contract of ecological disaster, as we will in time discover. By this spear he had subdued the giants but also on it he had confirmed payment for their labour.

Fricka complains that if she had known of his scheme she might have stopped him:

doch mutig entferntet	but slyly you men
ihr Männer die Frauen,	did your talking in secret,
um taub und ruhig vor uns;	and kept us women away;

Here is the first indication of the danger inherent in man's current separation of women from the affairs of society. Wagner's vision of 'the couple' has not yet become embodied. Here he indicates the contemporary bourgeois situation. The challenge is not to turn the woman into a man and invite her to become political but to have the courage to confront what women see in life and men are blind to – this is the issue. It involves both a sense of compassion and also a sense of reality. Man's will to power is fuelled by both inspiration and fantasy, without permitting the woman's will to power, fuelled by realism and compassion, man will destroy himself. Fricka accuses her husband:

Was ist euch Harten	Nothing is sacred,
doch heilig und wert,	you harden your hearts,
giert ihr Männer nach !	when you men lust for
Macht	might!

The conflict between the two is electrifyingly modern. For her part, Fricka admits that she wanted Walhalla to 'keep him at home' and prevent his adulteries. From his point of view he needed Walhalla as a base from which to rule the world. She in turn upbraids him for building a fortress and throwing her away, as she puts it:

Liebe und Weibes Wert	Love and woman's worth.

Wotan reminds her that in winning her he had to lose an eye. He is pinning his hopes on Loge solving the situation. Freia in panic is fleeing from the giants. Fasolt and Fafner, the builders of Walhalla, have come to claim their reward. Das Rheingold is overtly political, and nowhere more recognisably so than in the confrontation and social contract that exists between Wotan and the two builders. Without their physical power and their labour the great edifice indicating the gods' leadership of the world could not have been built, yet in the act of building it the actual weakness and vulnerability of the power nexus are revealed. It is not simply a matter of capital and labour, as Shaw suspected, but of state power and its dependence and duplicity. The masses build the great edifices which, by their existence confirm the enslavement and deception of the people. So it is possible to recall in this century how the great network of banking institutions were built in the capitals of the West where before they functioned from a small building in the City, Wall Street, or the Bourse, and so on. No doubt there were 'labour disputes' about the workers' pay, but nobody had the faintest idea that a tiny elite of world bankers and brokers were building their Walhalla from which they would indebt the whole world and rule it. It is this very 'deception' that we are about to have dramatised in this preliminary evening to the Trilogy which will then chronicle the results of the criminal duplicity of the gods.

Fasolt reminds Wotan that he rules by rules. The state takes its power from its empowering mechanism, the constitutional grid. It imposes law and thus allows dominance, yet it must at least be seen to abide by its own delimitations. This is the challenge to Wotan, yet beneath the industrial dispute lurks another motive. Fafner reckons that if they win Freia then the gods will be deprived of her youth preserving golden apples. They will become mortal and lose their power to govern, and that power will pass to the worker giants. So, no sooner has the Ring entered the arena of life's action than we see the gods (the dominant power group) menaced from the dwarfs on one side, Alberich and the mobilised Nibelungen, and on the other side by the giants. Loge's appearance takes us directly to the fateful decision which he proposes to solve the gods' problem, but not before he has expounded his views in the long and lyrical narrative which reveals him as a being of exceptional intellectual and emotional complexity. His discourse raises the issue of the Nibelung dwarf, Alberich, who is now in possession of the Ring which gives him power to conquer the world. Loge's detachment from the issue and his fascination with its implications underlines the growing involvement of the gods and giants. Loge, seems to be setting a trap for them, luring them into desire for the Ring. Wotan begins to dream of further power. Fricka sees a path to marital fidelity. The giants, especially Fafner, begin to realise that the Ring would give them more than they dreamed, both the immortality they sought from the golden apples plus the power they sought over the gods. They order Wotan to give them the gold, in the meantime they have Freia as hostage.

The gods, deprived of Freia begin to weaken and age. Loge bitterly and yet ironically points out that it does not affect him since he has not been ordained with immortality and so is free of the dilemma now facing the weakening force of the gods. This final physicalising of the gods' dilemma forces Wotan's hand. He orders Loge to take him to Nibelheim to follow Loge's advice that what has been stolen can be stolen.

The descent of Wotan and Loge into the depths of the Nibelheim gold mines is one of the most powerful and original moments in the Ring. Loge, as god of fire, represents the unfettered intellect, yet intellect deprived of moral values is far from being 'pure' intellect, rather it itself becomes cunning, pragmatic, and self-serving. Thus, in turning to Loge for rescue, Wotan has done exactly the same as Alberich in his choice of cunning as his passion to replace the love he has renounced. Alberich had longed for the power of the gods. Wotan longs now for the power of Alberich. Soon Alberich's longing to regain Wotan's power will bring down upon all of them the inevitable disaster. Yet without this common desire and corruption inside the two characters, Wotan and Alberich, the terrible cycle could not have unfolded.

In the dark tunnels of the gold mine Alberich torments his own brother, the dwarf Mime, who has been commanded to create for his new master the magical metal helmet, the Tarnhelm which bestows invisibility on its wearer. Alberich exults that with this new technical wonder he will be able to see his workers without their seeing him, spy on them and check on their activities. Mime had hoped to steal the Tarnhelm but had not realised what powers it held. While the narrative line of the action in the gold mine is pure fairy tale – the magic helmet stolen by Loge's simple ruse of challenging Alberich to display its powers of transformation, so that first he manifests as a dragon with Loge feigning terror until Alberich vainly displays its further power by answering the challenge to turn himself into a toad, upon which Loge promptly imprisons him – the scene itself is a key to the whole cycle containing as it does the full clear and overt definition of what is at issue in the central conflict of the epic. It is only today with text, C.D. and score that the modern Wagnerian can go into the profound thematic structure that informs not only the music but the work itself as a dramatic statement of the human dilemma.

Significantly, throughout the scene the musical motives unfold their complex inter-related character as key symbols and elements of the drama begin to coalesce in the next major event of the Prologue, the second theft of the gold, and the presence of the Ring itself. Mime explains that Alberich has forged the Ring from the gold:

mit ihm zwingt er uns alle,	that Ring makes him our master;
der Niblungen nächt'ges Heer.	we Niblungs are now his slaves.

The first powerful political dimension of the saga is in place. Alberich in his reaching for world power has enslaved his own race; they, like his own brother, are held ransom to the programme for world domination. Before, the Nibelungen had been a humble peasant people living a simple primitive existence, since the forging of the Ring they have found themselves all forced into the social project of gaining wealth through the mining of gold. The Ring also contains the power to identify where there is gold to be mined so that the world's resources of wealth can all be captured in the great scheme of expansion whose realisation demands the enslavement of the Nibelungen themselves.

Pointedly, Wotan asks what use the gold is to Alberich since he can buy nothing in the mines. In Nibelheim the gold is mined and stored.

Doch mit dem Hort,	Then with my wealth
in der Höhle gehäuft,	from the darkness I'll rise,
denk' ich dann Wunder zu	and be master of all
wirken.	things;

Thus the vision of the Nibelung is nothing less than the overturning of the whole society, the destruction of the gods' culture – not the taking on of the civilisation of the gods but its liquidation by a very specific means – to turn the values of the gods into nought by the simple mechanism of replacing them with one thing – greed for gold.

Mit Golde gekirrt,	Enchanted by gold,
nach Gold nur sollt ihr	your greed for gold shall
noch gieren.	enslave you.

In the desire for wealth, Alberich explains, first the men will submit and then the women who once mocked him and looked down on him. It is a powerful and serious political programme which nothing will be able to withstand since its control mechanism, the Ring, will ensure the enslavement of the world.

Habt ihr's gehört?	You have been warned!
Habt acht!	Beware!
Habt acht vor dem	Beware of my armies
nächtlichen Heer,	of night
ensteigt des	Beware the day when the
Niblungen Hort	Niblung's gold
aus stummer Tiefe zu Tag!	shall vanquish the world!

And it is by the Tarnhelm that Alberich will both make the Nibelungen the masters of the world and still hold them enthralled by his power to watch over them, know what they are doing, and control them when they deviate from his wishes. With it he is absolutely safe from any attack. Of course, he had not reckoned with Loge's sophisticated mockery, which tempted him to show off and fall for the trick which left him in his turn a captive slave. Roped and bound he is dragged in fury back up through the mine shaft onto the mountain tops where the gods live and await their destiny. The music of the ascent is even more ominous and threatening than that of the descent, for now the irresistible crime will be committed, trapping the greatest of the god-race into betraying the very system of rules by which he has governed.

By capturing Alberich, Wotan has taken command of the Ring. Alberich had envied Wotan and the gods their superior culture and its aesthetic grace, and by the Ring he had determined to destroy it having no hope of emulating it. Yet Wotan in his turn has longed for the same powers not to destroy, certainly, but to exalt the gods over all existence. One race wants power in order to let destruction rule, the other to let creativity rule, from one point of view opposites and yet from another they are the same, both egotistically bound to the lust for absolute power whatever its moral ambition may be, and it is this common factor that is the dynamic of their mutual disaster.

It is as though Wagner perceived the destruction of his society through this collision of inevitably attracted opposites, culture and anti-culture, creativity and a barren mechanism of control, the multiplication of wealth. One group, ambitiously creative, fascinated by the trappings of power and the pleasure of life, utterly disdainful of others as being inferior to their irrefutable superiority to which only philosophy proves an elusive captor (Loge, one of the gods and yet not immortal, the dangerous outsider who will have the last word!). The other group despised and oppressed, bitter and in their turn ambitiously destructive. Never able to be masters for driven by no creative urge they are left to embody what Nietzsche was to define as ressentiment – the implacable negative emotion. 'You are bad, so we, by that fact, are good.' Their driving force is the negation of their noble masters. The Nibelungen's only concept of power would be the repeated act of humiliation and punishment of the gods for having been powerful and for having rejected them. It is this emptiness at the heart of Alberich's being that gives him his true equipoise in negativity. Alberich is fulfilled, finds his true reality, not in his wealth but in his own humiliation and defeat. It is in the curse that Alberich enters his own dark spiritual kingdom. Just as his personal relationship with women is at its most intense in his curses upon the Rhine Daughters so his political identity is at its most powerful in his curse upon Wotan, and by extension all those who might enjoy what he had been denied, indeed even when he had possessed it he had not enjoyed it – enjoyment of wealth was deferred to a future which never came, for he had not only lived in the present of possession and increase of the means to pleasure.

Having acquired the gold by force Wotan then orders Alberich to hand over the Ring. Alberich's reproaches have their own logic which Wotan cannot deny.

Wie glückt' es nur
dir Gleißner zum Heil,
daß der Niblung ich
aus schmächlicher Not,
in des Zornes Zwange,
den schrecklichen Zauber
  gewann
dess' Werk nun lustig dir
  lacht!

How well it worked for you,
you sneering rogue,
that I the Nibelung,
in shame and distress
maddened by fury
gained the terrible
  magic
to give you a plaything.

Wotan is implacable. He must have the Ring. Alberich in his most majestic moment, true to his own nature invokes his curse on the Ring. Against the terrible malediction of the curse Wagner sets a massive and intricate sonority from the orchestra, weaving the so-called Nibelungenhass, Fluch (curse), Ring, and Wehe! (Beware!) motives. From this moment the drama moves rapidly to its violent climax and beyond to its superbly ambiguous end.

The giants return for their ransom. The gold is dutifully piled up to match the outline of Freia's body. One last gleam from her eyes shines through the pile of gold, to wipe it from the giant's sight requires the surrender of the Ring. Adamant, Wotan refuses to part with it. Out from the depths of the earth itself emerges Erda, the ancient earth goddess of wisdom, and mother of the three Norns who weave in a cosmic cloth the destinies of men as they emerge to be fulfilled. Erda warns

Wotan that this event presages a terrible future for the gods. She vanishes as mysteriously as she had appeared. Wotan is anguished, longing to question her more. Moved by the ominous warning Wotan makes his decision. He throws the Ring onto the pile of gold for the giants to take. No sooner has the Ring changed hands than the inescapable curse falls on its new owner. Fasolt, who has been in possession no more than a moment, is felled to the ground, murdered by his brother. In that moment Wotan realises that its curse too, must fall one day upon him.

Furchtbar nun   Fearful power
erfind' ich des Fluchtes Kraft! lies held in that fatal curse!

So it is that at the moment when the gods are ready to enter their glorious new hall of power, Wotan is introspectively longing to go in search of Erda for further guidance. His wife, Fricka, coaxes him now to take up his residence in their new palace; Donner, as if to ease the task, clears the air of all its ominous darkness with thunder and lightning. The sky changes and a radiant rainbow bridge lights the shining path to Walhalla. Wotan, captivated by the sheer magnificence of their new abode again invokes a future of dreams and plans come true and final victory. Loge, excluded from their company, observes coldly:

Ihrem Ende eilen sie zu,	They hasten on to their end,
die so stark im Bestehen	imagining themselves strong
sich wähnen.	and enduring.

Here, right in the prologue of the drama he expresses his desire to see the arrogant epoch of the gods brought to an end by his power of fire. He joins them as they move across the bridge, musing on their possible end. Then from below comes the exquisite and poignant lament of the Rhine Daughters begging for the return of their gold. Irritated, Wotan asks Loge to shut them up and with his usual irony he tells them that now they can no more bask in the reflection of the gold, the gods' new radiance will have to do for them. The gods laugh and cross over into Walhalla, but the Rhine Daughters have the last word.

Traulich und treu	Goodness and truth
ist's nur in der Tiefe:	dwell but in the waters:
falsch und feig	false and base
ist, was dort oben sich freut!	all those who dwell up above!

Das Rheingold ends in a way that indicates totally the revolutionary nature of the work. From the beginning there has been no illusion that at the end somehow the gods will get away with it, leaving the mortals duly sorted out with their tragic destinies while they sit supremely above in their great hall restored to glory after the crises are over. From the moment the gods set foot on their radiant bridge to enter Walhalla they are doomed. Their self-deception that all is and will be well is brilliantly clear to the audience through the quite modern (now, to us) way that Wagner lets us know through his astonishingly coherent orchestral language. The first music-drama in the series is itself merely the prelude to the vast panoramic tale still to be told, and it is exactly this experience that Wagner leaves us with – not that something has happened, or is dramatically over, but rather – that a dreadful tragedy is about to unfold and no-one will be able to stop it. The power of the whole work is not in our sensation that the characters are doomed, this is projected on the work by those who do not know it at first hand, but its power lies in our recognising just how people do act in their freedom with that inexorability that somehow we are powerless to deflect.

When the public leave the theatre, they leave it thrilled, for the effect of Das Rheingold is visceral and immediate, and among the people can be felt a most unusual sensation at the end of an evening in the theatre, perhaps unique, that of anticipation. He has prepared us and we are ready for the unfolding of his tale – the story of the human race.

DIE WALKÜRE

Die Walküre is the first drama of the epic. Immediately we are plunged into a world of warring factions, tribal loyalties, oaths, treaties and betrayals, but the title is 'The Valkyrie', and in this work Wagner brings us his great new figure, the culmination of all his reflections on womanhood – a theme that was in fact to pursue him all his life and be the one which he died expounding – his model for the future, the new woman, Brünnhilde. From a narrative point of view there is no doubt that Wotan is the central character of the Ring. It is his tragedy which we are presented with in Das Rheingold and it is its working out that forms the substance of the tale, but what we have to remember is that Wagner is not at all interested in telling an ancient folk tale for its own arcane value. He is passionately concerned in unlocking the structural secrets of the springs of political power and human action for the future, in order, we might say, to let the future happen.

Saying that this is a revolutionary work does not for a moment imply that it is a marxist tract. On the contrary, its claim is that structuralist power must be destroyed if there is to be new life. In that sense Wagner sets out to liberate the revolution, to restore the concept to its Beethovenian, and Platonic purity. If the issue of the Ring were the simple dismantling of power structures then Wotan could rationally have remained as the central character, with his and Walhalla's destruction being the tragic accomplishment matching the triumphs of justice to the tragedy of hubris in the original Greek mode. The whole edifice is structured on an Aeschylean model, a fact which has been brilliantly demonstrated in Michael Ewan's 'Wagner and Aeschylus', but this was not Wagner's goal, and it is the insistence of some people to see in the Ring a 'classical' drama that leaves them also dissatisfied with those vital elements which do not fit their viewpoint.

It should be understood right from the beginning, therefore, that the Ring has two planes on which it operates – quite apart from the responsive plane of our assimilating the musical statements – one the narrative of the unfolding of the curse of the Ring to its completion, and the other and more complex, the drafting of the project of the Übermensch. When we have surveyed the Ring from beginning to end we will find that this project spills out beyond the framework of the Ring itself, and it could be said that to grasp this project whole it would necessitate an over-view of the whole mature oeuvre from Lohengrin to Parsifal, with

Tannhäuser its Prelude introducing us openly inside the 'narrative world' of the opera to the author of the original legend of Parsifal, the final exposition of which is the completion of the project.

Unless we submit to the moral and emotional patternings of the story as they are presented to us, without hiding behind an irrelevant, while utterly intriguing scholarship which tries to 'explain' the Ring from a detailed study of its sources and Wagner's impressive mastery of them, we will fail to make the odyssey the author invites us upon, nor can we possibly find solace in the decision to take the Ring simply as a late Romantic extravaganza. The mythic framework itself, the revolutionary credentials of the composer both in his theoretical writing and historically in the Dresden Uprising, and the enormous task of over a quarter of a century which took composition to realisation on a special stage built particularly to house the work, all these factors demand that we approach the Ring with a vivid awareness that Wagner has situated his 'edifice' in the heady mountain air where three countries meet, philosophy, art and politics.

Die Walküre begins in the middle of a violent storm. The curtains rise to reveal a great ash tree in which a sword is embedded to the hilt. This tree is the roof-tree supporting the primitive structure of Hunding's dwelling. The first figure to make his appearance is a fugitive and a rebel. It is Siegmund. Hunding's captive wife, Sieglinde enters to find the stranger collapsed in front of the fire from exhaustion. As she revives him with wine he begins to unfold his history. The storm outside, the unwelcoming nature of the house, the deeply troubled spirit of the stranger, mixed with the enormous relief experienced by Sieglinde in finding a sympathetic human being, however gloomy, charge the atmosphere with enormous tension. Hunding is a powerful and brutal host. With Wagner's famed sense of dramatic economy we learn of past events which at the same time express the present drama.

The pattern of relations is bare and formal. Siegmund is an outlaw, nowhere at home. Sieglinde has been violated and forced into marriage with Hunding. Siegmund lost his mother and his sister disappeared. The battle that had brought him to Hunding's hut has been an almost ritual re-enactment of his primal loss. He had come upon a band of soldiers intent on capturing another woman and attempting to abduct her. He had fought until exhausted, in the end the girl had been slaughtered. Of course, he is in the house of the raiders and is immediately challenged by Hunding to do battle with him the next day once the night's law of hospitality has been fulfilled. Yet Hunding suspects more, having seen in Siegmund's eyes the glittering light of the snake, the same light that is in his wife's eyes, the inherited sign of the dragon slayers. Unarmed, Siegmund must prepare to fight. Sieglinde wills him to look to the embedded sword but he fails to see it. Left alone, he broods over his cruel fate, his mind racing, seeking a way out of his dilemma. He reflects that his father had promised him that in his hour of need a sword would be given to him.

Sieglinde enters, dressed in innocent white. Immediately she informs Siegmund that she has dispatched her husband for the night with a sleeping draught. The way is clear for them openly to express their passionate attraction. In a long narrative she tells Siegmund of Wotan's visit to their house – the one-eyed wandering stranger who haunts these dramas, so anguished and lonely, and far from the arrogant self confidence of the god in Das Rheingold – and of his plunging the sword to its hilt in the tree to be the reward of the one who can extract it. Unaware, either that it is a god or her own father, she nonetheless feels his affection reaching her in the bleak setting of her captor's hall. In a moving identification of her recognition of her father with that of her certainty as to the one the sword is destined for, her story echoes the same phrase, speaking of Wotan she says:

<table>
<tr><td>Mir allein
weckte das Auge
süss sehnenden Harm,
Tränen und Trost zugleich.</td><td>I alone
felt in those glances
sweet yearning regret
sorrow and solace in one.</td></tr>
</table>

And to Siegmund declares:

<table>
<tr><td>Ich weiss auch,
wem allein
im Stamm das Schwert
  er bestimmt.</td><td>I know too
who alone
can draw the sword
  from the tree.</td></tr>
</table>

Sieglinde hails him as her 'heiliger Freund' and he reciprocates, claiming the sword and the woman. Then, in one of those magical moments of pure theatre which Wagner seemed to create so easily, he links the elements outside the crude hut to the awakening passion in the young couple. A burst of wind throws the door open, frightened, Sieglinde pulls away from Siegmund, crying:

<table>
<tr><td>Ha, wer ging? Wer kam
  herein?</td><td>Ah, who went? Or who's
  come?</td></tr>
</table>

Siegmund's tender reply begins their love scene:

<table>
<tr><td>Keiner ging.
doch einer kam:
siehe, der Lenz
lacht in den Saal!</td><td>No-one went
but one has come:
see him, the Spring
smiles on our love!</td></tr>
</table>

Thus begins Siegmund's famous declaration of his passion for his sister. It is noble and heroic, tender and then passionate, ending with that surge of triumph which always makes for that particular quality that is Wagner's eroticism, so far from the infantile sweetness of Mozart or the self-conscious unity between the man and the woman in Verdi. With Wagner the erotic union is always won against all odds, at some mortal cost, a private victory over the political facts, as too, is erotic sublimation. As the two lovers begin to exult in each other and feel at last that they are, for the first time since childhood, no longer alone, at the same time they reach out to that lost childhood and discover each other, lovers now, to have been brother and sister then. It is this richness of reference and command of feeling that gives to Wagner such absolute mastery in handling his audience as he negotiates to them the experience of delight in sharing the sexual pleasure of the incestuous lovers. Giving poignancy to their snatched, illicit passion, is the task to be faced the next morning when Siegmund must fight Hunding, with a sword that has been awaiting him, the fatal gift of his own father.

The naming of Siegmund, which is the seal of their love, is intertwined with the naming of the sword Notung! Need – underlining the terrible vulnerability of the young warrior. With the sword triumphantly drawn from the tree, the ecstatic lover claims his sister bride and they fall on each other to consummate their love on the floor of the hut. From the first performance of the work the curtain has fallen on this gloriously uninhibited declaration of incestuous passion to the thunderous applause and approval of the public. Our admiration for Wagner's theatrical wisdom in placing such a scene in the ancient mythic past and for so irresistibly winning us with the ravishing music of the love scene must not deflect us from the much more important element in the story. Wagner was perfectly serious in his proposition that the brother-sister couple were the necessary element in the creation of the saving Übermensch. Soaked as Wagner was in Greek myth he was far from unaware that in his new hero who was to appear in the next work, and whose procreation the first act of Die Walküre celebrates, he had created a model known also to the ancient Greeks he so loved and studied in their original language. As Heracles, the heroic athlete, was the son of a god and a human mother, so too was Siegmund. And as the latter in turn fathered Siegfried, so did the former father that prototypical Übermensch, Prometheus.

So it is that right in the opening act of the tremendous story we have proposed to us the ideal parents for the new man. The first part of the biological model has been laid out. Sired from the elite of the rulers of the world, born to a new race of humans specially selected by Wotan – genetically paired brother and sister form the parents of the one who will set out to create the new heroism. The second act defines what the second determinant will be that the child will be born into the world at the cost of his mother's life, with his father already dead. The biologism of the new hero is a vital part of Wagner's legend, as it was a vital part of the theories of Nietzsche, whose Will to Power notebook leaves us in no doubt that a new man cannot be created simply by offering him new social concepts, however exalted. The genetic history must be consciously determined. The infantile rearing must be monitored. A stepmother would guarantee the child's freedom to encounter woman as more than a re-enactment of the infantile need, while the absent father would assure that the emergent ego would not have an impossible struggle in rejecting the paternal model before confirming its own original identity. In the Wagnerian assessment, as we shall see, the second of these is accomplished by a ritualised rejection of the absent father, but the 'search' for the never-known mother proves disastrous for, having 'reached' woman with Brünnhilde, he is driven to continue his erotic quest, enchanted by women but without a memory to fix his own woman's image to, so that the two might coalesce.

This is not a psychological theme, nor is the saga a mere psychological mapping of archetypal male and female forms, this would be to project onto Wagner's schema far too trite and banal a subject. Wagner's concern in all this is totally political, and his psychology in turn he views as having a genetic and historic foundation. It was this mode of thinking, which is the mode of narration, musical and textual, in the Ring, that was to become, in philosophical terms the mode of thinking presented by Nietzsche in his own highly original aphoristic manner in a series of works all created sequentially after the impact of the Wagnerian Weltanschauung had impinged itself on the young philosopher.

Of one thing there can be no doubt, each, in his own way had located the search for a new historical force of renewal outside the zone of existing political forces in the world, and even outside man as he then was emerging at the dawn of technology. Both had recognised the need for a new typology based on a new genetic and biological model. Both reached out beyond the optimistic view of Goethe, who saw education as a formative programme of humanising, in his master-work Wilhelm Meister, and they recognised, in what is

the birth of modern consciousness, that the form-
ation of the child is both genetic – racial is no
longer the point, that was the only term available in
Wagner's day – and infantile, in as much as the self-
image is based on the childhood imprinting.

This creation of the new hero is not only the
preoccupation of Wotan, Wagner invites us to
make it intellectually our own. It is a central issue
which will not be fully resolved within the drama,
yet the failure to resolve it will be in itself a superb
artistic vision, utterly satisfying and poetically true.
As to the resolution of the theme in its fully
thought out form, for that we must prepare
ourselves through the long initiatory journey down
the Rhine that lies ahead.

The second act of Die Walküre consists of
four powerful and intimate duologues followed by
a final scene of ferocious action. When one considers that the first act is almost totally taken up
with the long love scene between Siegmund and
Sieglinde and that the last act, following the
electrifying meeting of the Walküre sisters, is in
turn a long and intense confrontation between
Wotan and his daughter, it is astonishing how
Wagner sustains the atmosphere of a great saga.
The first music drama has its gold mines and its
giants, the third its forge, its dragon and its
mountain of fire, while the final work is crammed

with visual spectacle. It is the enthralling Die Walküre, nevertheless, that maintains this intimate and intense atmosphere of deeply personal conflict and encounter.

It is with these great duologues that Wagner finishes once and for all the operatic schema of flat narrative confrontations. With his motivic method in full flight he is able to render these duologues as enormously complex emotional and intellectual encounters trading in mature and deeply modern worlds of feeling and idea. Nowhere in Wagner's work is the great Norwegian more present than in Die Walküre. It is Ibsen sung. His task in Die Walküre is to give us his second major protagonist, Brünnhilde. With Brünnhilde, Wagner makes his final statement on woman. In Brünnhilde he resolves the dilemma of Isolde as in Parsifal, as we shall see, he solves the problem of Siegfried.

Elsa, Wagner's first model of the revolutionary woman, is still destined to a fatal love from which she cannot escape. She falls victim to the narrative sweep of events called politics. Yet already Wagner has realised that she lives more truly and intensely than Lohengrin and is his superior despite the heroic destiny of the Grail knight. The first stage in the evolution of this model woman is replaced by the second stage which offers us Isolde. Isolde is dynamically refreshing after the quietism of the enchanting Elsa. She has become the woman of initiative, and if she has to have only an erotic destiny, here, she chooses for herself the terms on which the tragedy will be played out. She selects not only her lover but in doing so also punishes her presumptuous enemy.

With woman's sexual freedom confirmed Wagner still did not see the way through to the next evolutionary step. He had already recognised that woman-into-man, that is the political woman, was a delusion, since she did not resolve man's initial dilemma of being nothing more than homo politicus himself. There remained one necessary step and that was the woman's entry into the world of power, not as a pseudo-man but as a woman with her own unique spiritual identity intact, active and no longer passive, and that meant transformative and not merely receptive. It was this great theme that he was to realise in his extraordinary creation of a quite new kind of woman who was herself, liberated, independent, and who held in her hands nothing less than the means of returning the world to its basic harmony.

The music that heralds and accompanies Brünnhilde, the motive of the Walküre sisters is exhilarating and dynamic. Here is a new and tremendous energy that seems to sweep away all before it. Brünnhilde announces the arrival of

Fricka. Her scorn for the wife of Wotan indicates how far she is from the role of the bourgeois woman which Fricka embodies so utterly. Wotan's daughter, and a Walküre sister, is a new breed, wild and free. Brünnhilde's brief appearance makes all the more marked the domestic wifely femininity of Fricka, bound to the politics of family, marriage and private morality. Yet it is this force which is about to conquer the leader of the gods in an encounter as brilliantly argued as it is passionately expressed.

Within the mythic framework Wotan and Fricka are immediately recognisable as the bourgeois couple, he faithless and pursuing political goals, she betrayed yet insisting that the principles of marriage and fidelity be given at least a formal recognition. Fricka, even as she dooms the attractive lovers, is enormously sympathetic, convincing, and this is the pathos, with no alternative but to destroy the illicit lovers to protect her own loveless situation from complete disaster.

With absolutely clear and inescapable argument she drives Wotan to accept that he cannot as the head of the gods whose power is based on law and morality permit an incestuous couple to get away with flaunting the moral law. She accuses Wotan of sexual adventurism, while he has seen himself as on a quest to find the right model for his new man who will save the world from the curse of the Ring, yet they have drifted so far apart that there is no explaining, no sharing possible. Hopelessly Wotan complains of her failure to comprehend and tries one last time to explain:

Nichts lerntest du	You never learn
wollt' ich dich lehren,	what I would teach you,
was nie du erkennen kannst.	to try to conceive a deed
eh' nicht ertagte die Tat.	before that deed comes to
Stets Gewohntes	Your concern / pass.
nur magst du verstehn:	is for things that have been
doch was noch nie sich traf,	but for what is still to come
danach trachtet mein Sinn.	to that turn all my
	thoughts.
Eines höre!	Hear this one thing!
Not tut ein Held,	We need a hero – who lives
der, leidig göttlichen Schutzes,	without our protection
sich löse vom Göttergesetz.	free from the rule of the
So nur taugt er	He alone / gods.
zu wirken die Tat,	can do the deed, which
die, wie not sie den Göttern,	though it will save us
dem Gott doch zu wirken	the gods are forbidden
verwehrt.	to do.

Scathingly, Fricka reminds Wotan that the humans are not free. On their own they can do nothing – they rely on this transcendental force that is the power of the gods. Here, by her inexorable logic, Fricka drives Wotan to confront the need for another sort of man who can act freely and spontaneously out of his own freedom and courage. With this we enter directly the domain of what is now thought of as Nietzschean thought, but the vision and the concept were themselves, in the first place, Wagnerian. The first step that Wotan has overtly taken to create the Overman, is also his second step towards the destruction of the gods themselves, his first having been the theft of the Ring. Once Fricka has confronted Wotan with the fact that Siegmund is not a free agent, but merely a tool of Wotan's, the young warrior's fate is sealed. There is no point in his victory, he cannot fulfil the role that Wotan requires. Bitterly he acquiesces to his wife and swears to her that he will fall in the battle, Wotan's protection withdrawn.

As Fricka departs in triumph Brünnhilde returns, aware that Wotan is profoundly distressed. In anguish the tormented god cries out over the orchestral storm:

O heilige Schmach!	Oh sacred shame!
O schmächlicher Harm!	Oh shameful affliction!
Götternot!	God's despair!
Götternot!	God's despair!
Endloser Grimm!	Endless remorse!
Ewiger Gram!	Grief evermore!
Der Traurigste bin ich von allen!	I am the saddest of all!

Shaken by her father's agony she lays her head in his lap and begs for him to confide in her. Responding to her tenderness and love for him Wotan lays bare his deepest feelings. This duologue between father and daughter, dominated as it is by his long, reflective narration, is one of the magisterial passages of the Ring, taking us into a quite new realm of human experience, combining political anguish with an intricate and moving psychology of father and daughter. In the world of the gods and Walküre we find ourselves in a human, all too human world with which we can immediately identify, and which speaks to us in a way art never had before of how what we had thought was our personal psychology was nothing other than the working out of events themselves. Here music is used to reveal the web of connections between the self's inner movements and the driving force of political action.

Right at the beginning of Wotan's long confessional he expresses his dilemma:

gewann ich mir dir Welt	I won myself the world
....	......
Von der Liebe doch	Yet the longing
mocht' ich nicht lassen;	for love would not leave me;

Wotan rules by a set of laws and contracts, yet it is

these, the source of his power, which prevent him from fulfilling his own yearning for love and even for absolute and thus lawless power. His own lonely search for knowledge and love takes him down into the depths of the earth to meet the Wala, Erda, who had so awesomely appeared to warn him of the curse of the Ring.

mit Liebeszauber   by love's enchantment
zwang ich die Wala,   I conquered the Wala,

So we learn that Brünnhilde and her eight sister Valkyries are the children of the Earth Goddess. Their role is to avert the oncoming disaster by gathering up an army of dead heroes from human battlefields and resurrecting them in Walhalla. Here Wotan reveals the gods' disturbing activity among mortals. The humans are controlled by sets of rules and agreements which curb their pride. They are afraid of the power of the transcendent forces of 'gods' and at the same time are roused to mutual self-destruction in 'ruthless war' in order to provide this new army whose task will be the defence of the gods' power against the insurgent dwarf uprising led by Alberich. Wotan's fear is that should the Ring return to the Nibelungen then even his host of warriors could not stave off disaster, through the Ring's power they would be induced to fight on the side of Alberich. Wotan cannot retrieve the Ring from Fafner or he would break the treaty system by which he rules.

Only a man who is free and an enemy to the gods, without fear, could perform the very act Wotan requires to save the situation. He realises the irony that if he creates a man he has by that token created not a free agent but a slave. Here is the crucial heart and core of the drama. Wotan, head of the gods, now needs to pass beyond the god-man contract in order that existence should survive and evolve. He has reached an end point of things as they are. He must now pass over into a new and unknown situation. He has reached the point at which there must be a transvaluation of those values which up until then have governed life. And from this need grew the idea of rearing a saviour among the Walsung. The most significant part of his education – in the creation of this new man – has been, not only his wildness and freedom, but his rebellion.

gegen der Götter Rat	I taught him to hate the gods,
reizte kühn ich ihn auf.	urged his heart to rebel.

It is at this point that he admits his failure. His free agent has only one means of survival, the sword put into his hand by Wotan himself. Fricka has unmasked the deception and left him no choice but to obey her insistence that the laws continue to be upheld. Now, the curse of the Ring working upon him, he finds he must kill the very son he loves. In anguish he recognises that all his ambitions are burned out, everything lies in ruins about him.

nur eines will ich noch: but one thing I desire:
das Ende, das Ende!   the end, the end!

His anguish is complete in the knowledge that Alberich has forced a woman to bear him a son:

des Gunst Gold ihm   compelled by
  erzwang   gold-credit

while he remains longing for the impossible 'Other':

Das andre, das ich ersehne, the Other I long for,
das andre erseh ich nie: that Other I can never find:
denn selbst muss der Freie for the free man must create
sich schaffen;   himself;

And so the knot of their destinies slips into place. Wotan who loves Siegmund commands his daughter to let him fall in the battle. Brünnhilde who loves her father is now placed in the position of her father's will, which she must execute. It is only a step and the love of daughter for father will become transformed into the love of daughter for father's loved one, his son. In so doing, the genetic incest of Siegmund and Sieglinde moves into the realm of symbolic incest, the pattern is complete. Brünnhilde is being asked to kill her step-brother.

She argues passionately with Wotan not to go through with the execution but he is ferociously insistent, warning of his terrible and implacable rage. With heavy heart Brünnhilde sets out to betray Siegmund.

Alone Siegmund and Sieglinde await the on-coming conflict, and while Siegmund exults in his new found sword, Sieglinde is filled with fore-boding and guilt about the outcome. Tenderly her brother and lover lets her rest exhausted as he guards her. A sombre music prepares us for Brünnhilde's arrival to inform the young warrior that his sword will be of no avail and that he will fall in battle. She has come to announce to him his place in Walhalla. Gravely, she informs him that there is no escape, she has looked upon him and this has sealed his fate. Unperturbed, Siegmund begins to question her about his destiny. He learns that in winning an honoured place among the dead heroes he must also be parted from his beloved. Calmly he informs Brünnhilde that he does not wish Walhalla at such a price for without Sieglinde it has no meaning for him. Brünnhilde is deeply disturbed by a reaction she has never encountered before from a hero about to die. He adamantly refuses the heroic eternity she offers him and even when told that his sword will not save him he refuses to concede. Brünnhilde's shock becomes snarled in deeper emotions. She has never before faced a man whose love is more valuable to him than his life. He tells her that he finds her cold and hard, but as he says it the young Walküre's heart is in turmoil. Brünnhilde's spirit reaches out and identifies with his suffering, just as Parsifal does with the wounded Amfortas. She steps over the line of self-interest and duty into the realm of love. Undertaking to defend him in the battle she says her farewell, a word that will soon resonate in her father's last words to her.

Leb wohl, Siegmund,	Farewell, Siegmund,
seeligster Held!	blessed hero!

The Second Act ends in an intense and abrupt series of events. Hunding emerges to do battle and for a moment Brünnhilde takes her place in defence of Siegmund but the sudden arrival of a furious and powerful Wotan shatters the sword in one blow of the god's spear. Siegmund falls dead. Brünnhilde escapes with Sieglinde, Wotan in his frustration also kills Hunding but his rage is for his disobedient daughter, the Walküre.

Act Three opens on the eight Walküre sisters of Brünnhilde gathering the dead from the battlefield to the accompaniment of their wild and whooping cries. Despite its familiarity and its frequent exploitation by others, in the theatre it remains uniquely dazzling and exciting. This vision of women as wild cosmic warriors came as a shock to its first public but it should not be under-estimated how much it still disturbs an audience, only now there are many more women open to enjoying the Wagnerian vision. Perhaps it would be appropriate here to remind ourselves of the different elemental projections of women which appear in the Ring. The Rhine Daughters are, of course, spirits of the waters, representing a delicious, frivolous sensuality. Carefree, they play and tease without any sense of the world, and when the gold is lost, they lament with the sorrow of innocence. The Walküre, riding the clouds, are of the air, vibrant and heroic, imbued with manly qualities, yet women. They know sisterhood, and when Brünnhilde is in trouble, against all wisdom, they defend her as best they can. The Norns are from the depths of the earth. They embody woman in her ancient wisdom and gravity. They know and they understand suffering, yet they remain helpless as men weave themselves relentlessly into their cloth of destiny. It is Brünnhilde who's element is transformative fire. Here, she is connected to Loge, the god of fire and intellect. It is intellect she wins at the end. Her tragic destiny begins when she is surrounded by the ring of Loge's fire as we see in this act, and she finds her liberation in the flames of Loge when at last they engulf the gods and set the world free.

At the tremendous reunion of the Walküre sisters, Brünnhilde tells of the battle and the need to hide Sieglinde. She decides on the forest where the dragon Fafner guards the Ring since it is forbidden territory:

Ihn scheut der Mächt'ge	Our Master fears it
und meidet den Ort.	and avoids the place

To encourage Sieglinde she announces to her that she bears Siegmund's child, as the orchestra declares for the first time the full and glorious motive of Siegfried.

den hehrsten Helden	the noblest hero in the
der Welt	world
hegst du, o Weib,	oh woman, you carry
im schirmenden Schoss!	in your womb!

Ordering her to guard the pieces of the shattered

sword she also reveals that her son one day will forge it anew. Brünnhilde then triumphantly names the unborn child: Siegfried – the victorious. Deeply moved, Sieglinde bursts out in praise of Brünnhilde, it is a moment of enormous unleashed emotion, all the more so because of the ambiguity that Wagner is able to bring to such moments by his motivic syntax, for we are to hear this ravishing phrase again, at the moment of the final apotheosis of the saga. That it should first declare itself on Sieglinde's lips at the annunciation of her child, Siegfried, the hero to come, is of the deepest import.

O hehrstes Wunder!   O sublime miracle!
Herrlichste Maid!   Glorious maid!

No sooner has Sieglinde gone, for the Walküre at the last moment do not dare disobey their father and Master, than Wotan in a towering rage appears. Brünnhilde presents herself with nobility and humility. He tells her that the love and the work between them is finished for ever. She is to be banished. Wotan informs her that he will put her to sleep on the rock and there she will lie until awakened, whatever man does so may claim her. To the Walküre Sisters the idea of being married to a mortal is horrific. Obedience and spinning by the fire – these are the terrible punishments to which

Wotan condemns Brünnhilde in the future. No one is to go near her. He orders the Walküre to ride away from the mountain, banished from their sister.

Thus, father and daughter are at last alone. The transitional music prepares us for their last moving encounter. It is another ambiguous and tortured duologue, more so than that between Wotan and his wife. Here the political reality of her disobedience to the head of the gods is mingled with the half expressed and only partly understood emotions of the protagonists. Brünnhilde reveals that love awakened in her heart for Siegmund and she desired to save him. Yet that love was 'engendered' by Wotan. In other words, she has transferred her love for her father onto the object of her father's love. In 'saving' Siegmund, she has performed the deed secretly desired by her father. To Wotan, on the other hand, equally enmeshed in the all-too-human trap, Brünnhilde has disobeyed her father. Underneath that, however, by her loving Siegmund in some deep way she has displaced her father and his love of her. As Fricka was jealous of both Brünnhilde and Wotan, so Wotan is now jealous of both Brünnhilde and Siegmund. His aggression in the same way is transferred from Fricka to Brünnhilde. In a sense, he is punishing the wrong person – but he cannot stop himself. It is this quality of a lovers' farewell which makes their parting more moving than that of Siegmund and Sieglinde. To ease the terrible cruelty of the sentence Wotan has imposed, or as he prefers it, she has brought on herself, Brünnhilde makes a request. She asks that the mountain should be ringed by fire so that only a hero, only a man without fear may be the one who will awaken her. Brünnhilde knows exactly what she is doing. Wotan does not wish to know. He only knows that he cannot come to the rescue of Sieglinde's child or he would in turn rob it of its freedom. Anguished, yet unable to stop himself, Wotan says farewell to his beloved Walküre:

Leb wohl, du kühnes,	Farewell, my bold
herrliches Kind!	wonderful child!
Du meines Herzens	My heart's holiest
heiligster Stoltz!	pride!
Leb wohl! Leb wohl!	Farewell! Farewell!
Leb wohl!	Farewell!

They say goodbye in a long embrace. He leads her solemnly, as in a trance, onto the rock. He takes away her immortality, lays her to rest, kisses her lips, and covers her with her Walküre shield. He strikes the rock with his spear and summons Loge to surround the rock with fire. As the flames leap up, and he confirms that now only a hero will be able to rescue her, the glorious music speaks to us not only of that hero who will come, but of that engulfing fire that awaits the gods.

SIEGFRIED

Wagner wrote that after the 'terrible tragedy' of Die Walküre he approached Siegfried 'with a sense of freshness such as I have never felt before'.[38] He got as far as the Second Act and spoke of it having given him a great deal of joy. The opera has been described as the tetralogy's scherzo, and this could be said up to that point where the Master laid down his pen, not for the year he imagined it might be but, in the end, for twelve years. Yet the interval – which in retrospect is all too understandable – was not only long and at the same time fecund – it was also at the right place in the saga to rest. The first two acts are the perfectly placed mid-section of the work. They are filled with vitality, scintillating energy, the dramatisation of the New Hero in all his physical dynamism and brutal force, and are a hymn to spontaneity and innocence.

It is with the Third Act, taken up after the long interval in which the composer, far from resting, composed his two other monumental masterpieces,

Tristan and Meistersinger, that we see the heroes, Siegfried and Brünnhilde, emerge from primal innocence into their encounter with the erotic drive. Since this subject, the human being's personality being pivoted on the erotic dynamism, was central not only to the Ring but the whole Wagnerian oeuvre, his rest from the great task at that particular point was, if not inevitable, at least appropriate.

Indeed, the composer returned to the task invigorated, and 'wonderfully in the mood'.[39] Fortunately, his own musical syntax guaranteed a sense of continuity to the work, since the motivic architecture remained constant and in place. Nevertheless his new musical expressiveness combined with a deeper understanding of his central theme gave to the Third Act its special power and emotional impact. Yet despite the inventiveness and energy of the work it remains, of the four dramas, the problem work. The problem is, without doubt, Siegfried. The matter is not clear – the total epic makes its absolutely resounding existence felt in the hearts and minds of the spectators. Despite much complaining, there is no doubt that the final ending is utterly satisfying and exalting. Even Siegfried himself achieves in his death what we are not too happy about in his life. Since it is utterly central to the narrative and to the philosophy of the work we must examine Siegfried further before proceeding.

There is little doubt about what Wagner wished to achieve with Siegfried and it is not that the character is difficult to understand, indeed, that may be just the trouble. He is not simply the noble savage, yet that is one aspect of him before his meeting with Brünnhilde and it is not there that the problem arises, rather, it is after that, when he must enter into a human maturity which is very much the central concern of the Ring. Let us set the character, or the persona, for to begin with he is deliberately devoid of self-awareness, within the framework of the epic. A race of giants and dwarfs inhabit the earth, ruled over by the superior race of immortal 'gods'. The race of the Walsung, the humans, become favourites of Wotan, since he sees in them a way out of the authoritarian pattern of life he is obliged to impose on others and which makes him its slave in turn. For the humans to be free they must be released from the fear of transcendent godly power, for, while it curbs their arrogance, it breaks their spirit. Behind that, however, is a deeper fear, the fear of death. In one sense all the characters are driven by this fear and as the composer observed in his key letter to August Röckel, 'We must learn TO DIE, and TO DIE in the fullest sense of the word; fear of the end is the source of all lovelessness, and this fear is generated only when love itself is already beginning to wane.'[40] The embodiment of this condition in its total sense is not Alberich, who is deliberately paired with Wotan in his drive to life – even his rejection of love is after being rejected! – but rather Loge, and Loge's only contribution to existence is the destroying flame, yet because Loge is also the intellectual he makes way for the future with his purifying fire. Siegfried's arrival in the epic is the coming of a man without fear. And while he is without fear, it cannot be said that he is without guilt, for he is deeply concerned that he may have been responsible for his mother's death in the crucial process of his own birth. He is without fear, yet in his discovery of Brünnhilde, to our relief it should be added, he does experience the sweet fear of man for woman, but in that complex and exciting scene he also matures in his immediate grasp that this fear is 'not fear' in the other darker sense, for it is dispelled by surrender and yielding.

From the political point of view, Wagner's major interest lay in the possibility of creating the new society on the other side of authoritarianism, which meant, structurally, the state. What he praised in Feuerbach, he himself desired, 'the radical emancipation of the individual from the pressure of inhibiting ideas associated with faith in authority.' Let us return to the Röckel letter of January, 1854. Referring to Röckel's imprisonment, Wagner raises the subject of freedom. It should be recalled that Röckel was serving a thirteen year term of imprisonment for his part with the composer in the Dresden Uprising.

> 'But what is freedom? Is it – as our politicians believe – 'licence'? – of course not! Freedom is: INTEGRITY. He who is true to himself, i.e. who acts in accord with his own being, and in perfect harmony with his own nature, is FREE; strictly speaking, outward constraint is powerless unless it succeeds in destroying the integrity of its victim, inducing him to dissemble and to persuade himself and others that he is a different person from the one he really is. That is true servitude... I believe that this 'integrity' is essentially the same as the 'truth' of which we read in books on philosophy and theology.'[41]

He goes on at length to explore this theme, pointing out that understanding reality is through the means of feelings, and distinguishes human from animal feelings, particularly identifying that capacity of the humans to recognise the mobile, fluid nature of existence, so that in the end they grasp that, 'only what changes is REAL.' This recognition, leading as it does to an abandonment of the search for the whole, brings about a new discovery in apprehending the process, and that is love. Since by definition the idea of understanding the totality or the concept is fruitless, it then is clear that love is not another abstract category but is itself all-too-human. 'Only as MAN and WOMAN can we HUMAN BEINGS really love, whereas all other forms of love are mere derivatives of it, originating in it, related to it, or an unnatural imitation of it.' He rejects the idea of higher forms of love alongside it. The highest form of satisfaction for the human ego is to abandon it, and that can only be done through love, and here he comes to his radical thought – 'only in the union of man and woman does the true human being exist, and only through love therefore do man and woman become human.' He insists that in love only does the union between man and woman, 'physically and metaphorically', create the human being. We will have to return to this at the end of the tetralogy. Our immediate concern is Siegfried, particularly before his crucial encounter with Brünnhilde.

About this, Wagner says: 'Siegfried is the man of the future whom we desire and long for but who cannot be made by us, since he must create himself on the basis of OUR OWN ANNIHILATION.'[42]

He adds another clue to his conception of Siegfried: 'In Siegfried I have tried to depict what I understand to be the most perfect human being, whose highest consciousness expresses itself in the fact that all consciousness manifests itself solely in the most immediate vitality and action.'

In this Wagner connects, consciously, modern man with Wotan, and so he implicitly defines modern man as standing in the way of the coming man. The vital difference between modern man and the coming man as understood by Wagner is clear. Modern man is the accomplice of the intellect (Loge), both in his social project (Walhalla) and its giantism (Fafner and Fasolt), as well as the accomplice of the usurers (Alberich), for without them payment cannot be deferred. Ruling by law and authority, law itself becomes a tyranny, and authority a deception. Modern man (Wotan) ends up the helpless slave of his own social process in its totality. The brilliance of the concepts (Loge's tricks), the cynicism of the law (Fricka's morality), the cruelty of the just social order (Siegmund's death), the inaccessibility of real wealth (Fafner sleeps on the gold), the enslavement of usury, (everyone is under the curse of the Ring, no-one can benefit from it), these are the conditions of the human situation.

It follows that the new man must embody

those forces which are the opposite of this intolerable stasis. Based as he must be on the acceptance of the underlying metaphysical truth (authenticity, in Heideggerian terms, integrity, in Wagnerian terms) that reality is pivoted on change, he must embody within himself that capacity to live in the present and be susceptible to the moment and its reality so that he will never ossify into the stasis that leads to the disaster of calling for social structures which embody fixity and thus the authoritarian outward law which ends with tyranny. If a man has chosen to be lawful, Wagner elsewhere points out, what use is the state to him, for he will embody it? Wagner never asks for anarchism in the modern and altered sense of the word following the triumph of the statist marxist dialectic. Rather, in this he remains an original Bakuninite, in asking man to choose to be self governing. Wagner's inescapable point is that such a self governing individual cannot result purely from some new kind of psychology, but can only come about by the destruction of the old order and the old type of person – because they have no choice but to destroy such a new kind of human and no other response to its emergence. This is the decision of Wotan – to make way for the future. This is the tragedy of Siegfried – to be destroyed by liberation politics (Hunding and the emergent Gibechung).

And so it is that while the problem of Siegfried has to be confronted, it is not insoluble if viewed from the Wagnerian viewpoint. What again we cannot fail to observe is how immersed in 'Nietzschean' thought is the ethos of the Ring, and therefore, since it precedes the corpus of the philosopher's work, how Wagnerian is Nietzsche. And at the same time we should not fail to recognise how much both of them derive radical new understanding of life from Bakunin's dynamic existence. Shaw, it will be remembered, called our hero Siegfried-Bakoonin.

Wotan, constantly throughout the cycle is announcing the coming of the new man just as Zarathustra announces the coming of the Übermensch. Zarathustra comes down from the mountain just as Wotan descends from Walhalla. Zarathustra and Wotan both name themselves the Wanderer and go in search of knowledge. Thus Übermensch is not to be seen as some kind of solution to the future of human history, this is why Nietzsche's doctrines are so often misunderstood. He is not an evolutionist, while not denying change as the underlying impulse of life. He is proposing another view of existence which involves a post historical consciousness while rejecting the cyclic view of primitive seasonal change. His doctrine of the Eternal Return involves a qualitative grasp of existence which implies that we are always coming upon the abyss of annihilation at every moment and not just that of death, not just in our lives but in our epoch so that what was once historicity itself becomes bonded into our own existential pattern. It is this view which Nietzsche proposes as the release from the disaster of transcendentalism and its accompanying Platonic yearning for the Utopian solution. This is the foundation of his anti-statism, and his anti-religion. His famous 'god is dead' is nothing other than the major news of the Ring. When theism is abolished, it follows logically, so too is atheism, and this is the heart of the matter. The human affair is not to be grasped conceptually but only in vision and metaphor. Human historicity is matched by Darwinian biology, and here Nietzsche makes his own unique contribution to current understanding. He opposes the Darwinian viewpoint precisely for its linear thinking, its implied sense of forms moving to some kind of perfection through the correction of minor weak-nesses in the species at a pragmatic survivalist level. He, and he alone, saw the dangers of the inevitable 'social Darwinism' that did of course and does dominate this epoch.

In 1888 in 'The Will to Power' he wrote: 'What surprises me most when I survey the broad destinies of man is that I always see before me the opposite of that which Darwin and his school see or WANT to see today: selection in favour of the stronger, better constituted, and the progress of the species. Precisely the opposite is palpable: the elimination of the lucky strokes, the uselessness of the more highly developed types, the inevitable dominion of the average, even the SUB-AVERAGE types. If we are not shown why man should be an exception among creatures, I incline to the prejudice that the school of Darwin has been deluded everywhere.

> 'That will to power in which I recognise the ultimate ground and character of all change provides us with the reason why selection is not in favour of the exceptions and lucky strokes: the strongest and most fortunate are weak when opposed by organised and herd instincts, by the timidity of the weak, by the vast majority... Strange though it may sound, one always has to defend the strong against the weak...'[43]

This last statement describes the tragic dimension of Siegfried and the end of the Ring. It is wrong to ask of Siegfried the characteristics of Wotan when it is precisely these elements in his psychology which doom him and the gods. Yet Siegfried is only possible through Wotan's surrender of his own power by choice. He, as we shall see, quite literally makes way for Siegfried. It is Siegfried's recognition of the meaning of that act which gives him his power as well as his failure to recognise it historically. If he had identified Wotan as his progenitor, and been trapped in the inevitable human 'pity', then the next phase of life could not have taken place. Siegfried's cruelty is a necessary part of his dynamism. His killing of Mime is 'Darwinian' survival but his actions after that are pure demonstrations of the will to power.

From a Wagnerian – and Nietzschean – point of view Siegfried is 'everything we are not'. He is not inhibited from action by moral introspection. He is not a thinker, not in quest of knowledge, not a moralist. He is spontaneous, virile, enthusiastic, passionate, trusting. He is the opposite of all that Nietzsche defined as the decadent personality, the 'civilised' creature. He is not the Rousseau Noble Savage at all, simply because he is not content to remain under the primitive rule of the seasons and procreation. He is the Übermensch, or, and here we come to that distinctive Wagnerian element in him, he is half the Übermensch, awaiting fulfilment in union with Brünnhilde.

Unless the physicality and eroticism and power of Siegfried are present in its interpreter the music-drama simply cannot work. The mythic significance of the hero is dependent on his presence in the work embodying not only his nature but his 'glorious' appearance of which both Nietzsche and Wagner openly spoke. The truth of the matter is that we have not yet seen the Ring produced with an appropriate Siegfried.

The first act opens in the forest where we find Mime, the guardian of the young Siegfried. Mime is Alberich's brother, and he is biding his time until he is able to forge the sword from its fragments and send the young Walsung out to kill the dragon, Fafner. Yet each time he forges the metal it breaks in two. Siegfried's first appearance confirms immediately his wildness and force. He enters driving a wild bear into their cave to the horror of Mime. On being asked why he has done this he immediately answers:

| Nach bessrem Gesellen | I was looking for a |
| sucht' ich, | better companion, |

so the first thing we learn of Siegfried is his loneliness. While Mime plays the role of the fond guardian Siegfried stubbornly refuses to play the dutiful role of grateful orphan.

| Doch was du am liebsten | but what you most sought to |
| mich lehrtest, | teach me |

> zu lernen gelang mir nie: I never managed to learn:
> wie ich dich leiden könnt'   how to tolerate you.

Despite Mime's claim that he is both father and mother to the boy, Siegfried is not convinced. His observations of nature lead him to another conclusion, and it is this that awakens the turmoil in his heart. Driven by his desire for self-knowledge Siegfried forces out of Mime a confession that he is in fact the orphan child of Sieglinde who died giving birth to him. His inheritance is only the shattered sword. Urgently he insists on his desire to forge the sword:

> Aus dem Wald fort   Through the wild world
> in die Welt ziehn: I shall wander,
> nimmer kehr ich zurück!   nevermore to return!

Siegfried rushes out leaving the desperate Mime wondering how he can forge the fragments of a sword which seems unmendable. Wotan enters, cloaked, with a large hat hiding his missing eye. Now, he is no longer the great god of Rheingold, but the anonymous Wanderer, roaming the earth in search of knowledge. Observe that where he seeks to understand the meaning of the whole cosmic situation, Siegfried passionately desires nothing more than to know 'who' he is.

The Wanderer observes to Mime:

Mancher wähnte	Many imagine
weise zu sein,	wisdom is theirs,
nur was ihm not tat,	but what they most need
wusste er nicht;	they do not know;

Wotan speaks from his experience. He needed at one point to forge the sword. Siegmund then needed to wield it. Now to escape the forest and meet his future, Siegfried needs to forge it anew. The name of the sword is Notung – need! In the end Wotan will need it again to shatter his own spear and power over men.

Mime puts three questions to the visiting sage. What race lives in the depths of the earth? What race lives on the face of the earth? What race lives above the clouds? The Wanderer gives his answers, the Nibelungen, the giants and the gods. Then he in turn insists on posing three questions to Mime. Wotan asks a different kind of question. He asks: what race did Wotan, although he oppressed them, most love? Mime answers, the Walsung. What sword must Siegfried use to kill the dragon? Again he gives the reply, Notung. Lastly, he asks: who will weld the pieces of the shattered sword? To Mime's horror he realises he does not know the answer. Wotan reminds him that his questions were all about distant, abstract things. His need was right in front of him, and he did not ask about it. Now Wotan gives him his answer in an enigmatic form:

Nur wer das Fürchten	One who has never
nie erfuhr,	learned to fear,
schmiedet Notung neu.	will make Notung new.

Mime realises as he converses with Siegfried that while he knows nothing of fear, and thus may forge the sword, if he is afraid of the dragon he will be of no use to him, yet if he is still fearless and kills the dragon he too will be in danger. So he constructs his plot to fulfil his ambition. Siegfried will kill the dragon and win the Ring and the Tarnhelm, then while exhausted from his labours, Mime will give him a drink of herbs which he will have prepared, and poison him, and so gain the treasure. As Siegfried sets about the business of forging the sword with thrilling zest, Mime is lost in his dreams of revenge and control. Once the treasure is his, his next act will be to kill his own brother, Alberich, who first set him on the trail of the Ring, and yet who treated him so cruelly. Already he sees himself as the ruler of the Nibelungen. Even as he dreams of the future, Siegfried has forged the sword and with a great sweeping blow he tests it on the anvil which splits in two.

Act Two opens with the second of the four dramatic encounters of Wotan-Wanderer. This time he confronts his arch-enemy, Alberich. He calls him Black-Alberich and opposes to him his own identity as Light-Alberich, not so much to suggest they are alike, apart from their desire for the Ring, but rather to suggest they are opposites. Wotan is a Master, Alberich is a Slave. He is trapped in his slave psychology and so, according to Wotan, he cannot win. Of course, Alberich immediately recognises his antagonist. He taunts Wotan with his dilemma, and warns him that when the Ring falls to him:

Walhalls Höhen	Walhalla heights
stürm ich mit Hellas Heer;	I'll storm with hell's hosts:
die Welt walte dann ich!	then I'll rule the world!

Cleverly, Wotan unsettles Alberich by pointing out to him that there are two Nibelungen who want the Ring. Fafner will surely be killed and then whoever wins it, wins it. Ironically he suggests Alberich warn the giant and recommend he surrender the Ring to save his life. Fafner is not interested. Wotan then declares to his enemy the heart of his own newly won wisdom.

Alles ist nach seiner Art,	Everything goes its own way,
an ihr wirst du nichts	you can alter nothing.
ändern.	

It is not determinism, not fatalism, but his own recognition that individual acts of freedom cannot be other than inevitable, and that the web of event and personality condemn one to freedom. What his secret is, is that only the one who chooses the inevitable is truly free. This is the Schopenhauerian core of the Ring saga, but where Wagner fundamentally and consciously differed from his revered teacher was that he did not see this situation as pessimistic but as enormously releasing, and a source of power. Here again Wagner and Nietzsche interpret nihilism with an exhilarating sense of liberation, and it is this triumphant relief that we are to experience at the utterly destructive finale to the tetralogy.

Mime leads Siegfried into the Neidhöhle forest. While Mime is comically wishing that his young hero and the dragon would kill each other Siegfried is musing on his parents. Yearningly, and exquisitely, he evokes the moment of recognition between mother and son. The Waldvogel sings her birdsong tantalisingly to him but he cannot make sense of it. Finally, arrogant and ponderous, the great dragon emerges from its lair to confront the one who summonses him with his eloquent horn. Siegfried plunges Notung into the dragon's heart up to the hilt. While the dying dragon tries to warn him of the danger he is in from Mime his only thought is to ask Fafner if he knows where he came from, but the dragon dies simply echoing back his name, 'Siegfried!' At that moment he puts his finger in his mouth to suck the blood spilt by the dragon. That drop of blood gives Siegfried the power to understand the birdsong of the Forest Bird. The Waldvogel explains the significance of both Tarnhelm and Ring yet Siegfried seems scarcely to grasp what it means.

Alberich and Mime meanwhile fight each other over the trophies. Cursing each other in the manner of the Nibelungen, they only succeed in hating each other more ferociously. Siegfried emerges bearing both the Tarnhelm and the Ring which on the advice of the Waldvogel he has taken as souvenirs of the encounter. Then, as Mime plots the death of his ward, the Waldvogel explains to Siegfried what his real thoughts are behind the sweet words he speaks. Helplessly trapped in a comic situation which reveals his lethal guile, Mime is justly rewarded with a swift thrust of Notung. The Ring has claimed two further victims, and now it is fatefully in the hands of the hero.

Siegfried confides in his new friend, the Waldvogel, that now he is all alone. He is told that a bride awaits him. She lies sleeping on a rock awaiting the man with the courage to penetrate the flames and awaken her. The curtain falls with Siegfried rushing to Brünnhilde and the inevitable.

Act Three belongs, as Carl Dalhaus has observed, along with Götterdämmerung, to the sombre and noble end of the saga. The 'scherzo' in the forest is over and now Siegfried becomes a man and faces his destiny. The action begins with the dark and introspective duologue between Erda and Wotan. Since the profound and challenging warning Erda had issued him when he took the Ring, Wotan has wandered the earth seeking knowledge and meditating not only on a way out of his dilemma but also the meaning of it. Erda tells the Wanderer to seek enlightenment from Brünnhilde, who being the child of Erda and Wotan is both brave and wise. Anguished, Wotan begs for guidance. It is Erda who has taught him fear so she must help him. Confused at his rejection of Brünnhilde, the earth mother has no word of comfort. Deep in his being this last chance of a political solution or a rational comprehension being denied him awakens a new strength. His fear leaves him. Wotan gives the future to Siegfried, convinced that his nobility will conquer the slave mentality.

Wachend wirkt	On waking
dein wissendes Kind	the child of your wisdom
erlösende Weltentat.	will perform the act that frees the world.

He confirms, too, that his beloved Brünnhilde will be the one who liberates the world from the curse of the Ring. In ceding his godly authority he passes it to the young, an instruction to be obeyed by theatre directors in their casting of the singers!

With the disappearance of Erda and the arrival of Siegfried the action reaches Wotan's last appearance in the epic. His brooding presence will be felt throughout the final drama, but it is here that he makes his farewell to Siegfried and the world he ruled. Wotan's scrupulous care not to aid the young hero in any way is made all the more moving by his last defiant resistance which almost steps over the bounds to put him once more into conflict and the will to power. In the end he sustains even insult as the young man mocks his age and his absurd appearance. The music richly expresses the ambiguity of Wotan's situation and his yearning to reveal his identity to the one who is the means by which the world will be freed. But the music also reminds us that the pivot of action has indeed swung to Siegfried and at the last Wotan, his spear shattered by Notung, is almost swept aside by the force of the young man's passionate am-bition to find his new bride and companion.

With the last scene we enter fully into the realm of Wagner's mature music which will irradiate the final phase of his tetralogy. With Tristan and Meistersinger behind him the composer has entered into full magisterial command both musically and psychologically. Apart from its sheer beauty it is also enormously difficult for the singers to accomplish, demanding not only genuine acting ability but sheer stamina and the kind of voice that does not lose its tonality under pressure. It is this vocal spaciousness that is most difficult for the Wagnerian singer, it is not just a matter of noble pacing but rather of breadth inside the note. The stridency of which Wagner is sometimes accused is not due to his music but a lack of it, and it is in that Himalayan range of music which stretches from this last scene to the end of the epic that we find singers collapsing for lack of voice and breath. Along with the need for this vast open sound inside the note is required also that effulgent energy which is the key to Wagner's music as well as his philosophy.

And so Siegfried passes through the flames, removes the Walküre shield, and undoing the breast-plate, kisses his bride to life. Brünnhilde awakens, gloriously hailing the light. Once Siegfried has clarified that he has not awakened his mother he wastes no time in responding to the enormously erotic adventure of finding a magnificent woman alone on top of a mountain. So ecstatic is he, he fails to ask Brünnhilde what she means by a most important observation she makes:

Dich liebt' ich immer;   I loved you always

<table>
<tr><td>denn mir allein</td><td>for I alone</td></tr>
<tr><td>erdünkte Wotans Gedanke.</td><td>divined Wotan's thought.</td></tr>
</table>

Each in turn expresses fear of the other and then with a passion of enormous physical vigour and abandon the two lovers throw aside all restraint and fling themselves enthusiastically into mutual arousal. So enthralled is Brünnhilde that in her inspiration she glimpses the future.

<table>
<tr><td>Götterdämm'rung</td><td>Twilight of the gods,</td></tr>
<tr><td>dunkle herauf!</td><td>– your darkness fall!</td></tr>
<tr><td>Nacht der Vernichtung,</td><td>Night of annihilation,</td></tr>
<tr><td>neble herein!</td><td>– your mists descend!</td></tr>
</table>

Despite the climatic ecstasy of their song love and death are coupled in their final words as the curtain falls.

GÖTTERDÄMMERUNG

With the towering achievement of the last drama in the cycle the story of Alberich's Ring is brought to its devastating conclusion, the rich motives are woven together in their ultimate and most complex patterns, and the deep meaning of the whole epic shines through the final scene of destruction filling its spectators with profound emotion as they contemplate a new beginning.

The naked political conflict between gods, dwarfs, and giants which opened the narrative in Das Rheingold has now spread out across existence infecting all the peoples of the earth. Let us recall that from the first the crisis brought about by the theft of the Ring was deeply involved in the erotic drives of the protagonists. Alberich himself robbed the Rhine Daughters while roused to a fury of humiliation and sexual frustration. If they had succumbed to his advances he might have sunk voluptuously into the Rhine and 'history' would never have happened. The transformation of his erotic urge into a political one is the first unfolding we have of the springs of human action in the Ring. Wotan is unfulfilled and unloved, Fricka embittered by her husband's adulteries and scornful of his lust for greatness, the giants clumsily dream of a beautiful goddess as their prize for labour, Loge is scorned and unaccepted among the gods despite his brilliance. Each in his own way is trapped in the blocked energy of eros unexpressed. It is when Alberich makes the jump from an overtly erotic goal to a political goal that events begin to move. It is in the cross-over which diverts erotic energy into political drive that the drama is unleashed. After that, even withdrawal into a purely erotic world is no defence. The political forces destroy lovers almost as a by-product of their main function. Siegmund and Sieglinde are doomed, as is every character in the cycle who seeks erotic fulfilment. Siegfried's search for the companion who will end his loneliness is what leads directly to his destruction.

The fourth drama brings together a group of individuals each in their way thrusting after sexual encounter and it is the entwining of this intense sexual activity with the equally ferocious political scheming that plunges their whole society into its final destruction. The catalytic element in the ultimate crisis is Alberich's son who has taken his father's cursing hatred to another level of energy which has totally erased the erotic drive in any recognisable form. He is the final man in the historical cycle who seeks the Ring and the last to perish by it. His end brings the end. The utterly non-erotic man is by his own nature self destroyed, and what he desires is unattainable. Each of the protagonists fulfils its contract by losing love, only Hagen is unable to do so since he does not love anybody thus his reaching out for the Ring is itself suicide, so that we could say that his only love was for himself and it was that which the Ring finally claimed.

There is no escaping the political dimension of the Ring and its obvious view of wealth and power. The Ring as a metaphor for usury is vividly clear. It is not the gold which gives power, but the hoarding of the gold and the distribution among people of the Ring which gives the illusion of power and wealth but denudes its holders of life itself. The Ring is never USED. It renders possession a purely symbolic value. Sexual possession planes over into wealth possession and it in turn yields to power possession in its abstract form – the Ring. Wagner raises a fundamental issue related to Proudhon's 'property is theft' formula. Is there legitimate 'property'? Wagner seems to insist that the only legitimate property is the earth's own. Primal harmony, at least, is based on the gold being in the Rhine where it belongs. The Ring itself is a theft, as is the taking of interest.

What prevents the Ring from having a materialist and didactic viewpoint is Wagner's complex and convincing observation about this connection between social politics (including wealth) and the human psyche. As we have noted, there is no way to a new kind of human being unless the social framework in which he is located is itself first swept away. This was the political position of Bakunin whose presence haunts the Ring as much as he does the modern epoch. It should not be forgotten that the 'idea of Bakunin' of today is the product of a basically dominant marxist ethos and it offers history a romantic who wished to destroy all necessary and rational structures and set up a kind of infantile primitivism in their place. The Bakunin of Wagner is not that man. The famous battle between Marx and Bakunin resulted in the marxists putting out a version of what Bakunin believed which guaranteed that he would have few followers; this rewriting of history was to become a normal technique in the statism that emerged from the marxist methodology. The abolition of statism was simply taken off the agenda.

To relocate the meaning of Wagner's Bakunin – and it should always be remembered that Wagner's expressed sympathy with communism must not be taken to be an acceptance of marxism-leninism but rather that brand of revolution propounded by Bakunin – it should be recalled that prior to the domination of marxism there still remained a genuine European revolutionary ethos. That ethos did not express itself in terms of class war and expropriation by the workers, let alone a dictatorship of the proletariat. It was a genuine and profound re-appraisal of values whose motivating urge was towards liberation and spiritual life. We have already suggested that this movement which accompanied the scientific awakening of the eighteenth century and which contained in it a rejection of judaeo-christian values was highjacked by forces which emerged during the upheaval of the french revolution. Hopes were raised high by the Napoleonic counter-revolution but he too succumbed to the monarchic illusion and familial tyranny, giving up his struggle against the monetarist forces he had tried to overthrow. As the monarchies collapsed, the banks phoenix-like arose from the ashes of the old order while under the guise and name of revolution a scenario was played out which made possible that very social transformation.

The aristocracy and the great families, as well as christianity in Europe and Islam in Turkey, were all broken in fragments. The empires fell, the french, the russian, the german and the turkish, and in their place came monetary power structures. Wagner found himself as it were in the first act of the tragedy, that is, from the french revolution up to the 1884 uprisings. A dialectic was being worked out which was still functioning successfully in 1968. By now the pattern is almost complete and it is possible to see many of the things Wagner and his contemporaries most dreaded as having come about. Certainly the power of interest-capital to enslave mankind in a global system of debt from which it cannot escape, a debt owed to an oligarchic minority unbounded by the state and elected by no known franchise, is now the fundamental fact of modern life.

In 1876 Edward Grieg, the Norwegian composer, wrote of the Ring: 'This strange work, summing up the whole of our present culture, has an added strangeness in being so far in advance of our time.' Now, over a hundred years later it is beginning to emerge as urgently relevant. It is of our time. While in his theoretical writings he thrashed about trying to find a firm political position to embody his revolutionary spirit, sometimes hitting the mark with astonishing exactness and at others falling for postures which today seem inevitably outmoded, it is as an artist that he demands to be judged and it is in the Ring that he leaves his political testament. The composer of the Ring was a man who could write, over a hundred years ago, of looking forward to the day when 'this demonic concept of money will leave us, with all its frightful retinue of overt and covert usury, bond-swindling, interest, and bankers' speculations.'[44] He unequivocally declared himself for a future world with 'one religion and no state'.[45] Most of all, he had no doubt but that man had to counter-balance the erotic drive, not by repressing it but by transforming it. Short-circuited it became politics and in the place of desire came force and the creation of the imprisoning state. The rules and contracts of power politics, so just and noble sounding when first pronounced – like the American Constitution – become themselves the instrument of tyranny. The loveless, driven egos collaborate in mutual destruction. In other words, he sought the new man. The new man and the new society – Wagner stood between his two one-time friends, who in themselves embodied theoretically the radical position towards each of these issues. Bakunin stood for the destruction of the old order and the creation of a new one liberated from the inhibition of the structuralist state, while Nietzsche stood for the genetically redesigned new man who would be reared without the repressive imprinting of the old morality, the Übermensch. While Wagner translated Bakunin's concepts into mythic and musical language, Nietzsche also in turn translated his early master's artistic vision into a philosophical discourse.

To tackle these great subjects in artistic terms Wagner took the revolutionary Beethovenian music-al tradition into a further stage of its expression, claiming music to be 'a new language' which 'expresses just that which cannot be spoken by ordinary language.' It is the music which communicates to us another message, one that is not in the text, nor even on the stage, despite the now frenzied attempts of directors to de-Wagner Wagner on the one hand by reverting to an outdated literalism or on the other by projecting the whole drama into outer space or suspending it in a psychic void. It is the music which has been revealing to us, with its complex sonorities and its syntactical array of motives woven and interwoven, transformed and commented upon and drawn together, with its ever richer sonority which climaxes in the Götterdämmerung, deeper and deeper meanings as we arrive at understanding Wotan's tremendous thought the working out of which has dominated our lives for those four tremendous nights in the theatre.

Musically, the Prologue links us directly with the end of Siegfried but before we return to the lovers Wagner takes us even deeper into the mythic foundations of action. The Norns, daughters of Erda, spin the web of human destinies. They do not make destiny happen but rather spin the pattern of unfolding events like recorders of a chronicle yet to happen. The First Norn recalls how they once had spun their cloth at the world's ash tree, central force of the world's wisdom. Wotan came, forfeiting an eye to drink at the well of knowledge – by this he had won Fricka as wife – then broken a branch from the cosmic tree to carve his spear of runes and laws. The wound had weakened the tree and eventually it had decayed and died. The Second Norn adds a significant piece of news when Siegfried thrust Wotan aside and split his spear:

in Trümmer sprang   in fragments fell
der Verträge heiliger Haft.   the sacred register of
                                   contracts.

So it is that Siegfried's new found freedom means that he now moves in a world without laws or prohibitions. No external restraint remains on men's actions, it is into this ethos the drama now plunges us. Meanwhile, Wotan has had the heroes of Walhalla cut the dead wood of the primal ash and pile it around the great hall. The world-tree has fallen and the spring of wisdom dried up. When the logs around Walhalla are lit it will mean the end of the gods forever. The Third Norn adds that Wotan himself will use his shattered spear as a torch to set alight the logs around his hall when the time comes. As they spin out the actions of the future to find when that will be they come upon the curse of the Nibelungen's Ring. They ask what will become of it – and the rope of destiny snaps. They descend into the earth. History has come to an end.

On the rock Brünnhilde and Siegfried awaken ecstatically from their night of love. Siegfried, ready to set out for further adventure says his farewells to

Brünnhilde. He gives as a gift the Nibelungen's Ring. Enchanted with her 'sole possession' she gives to him her horse, Grane. They say a triumphant farewell to each other, confident of the power of their love. Siegfried journeys down the Rhine.

With Act One we enter the dangerous modern world which has left behind the old laws of honour and morality. Only lip service is paid to them, in fact, it is an existence of obsessive power politics, with the Gibechung people dominated by the half-Nibelung Hagen, the bastard son of Alberich, his step-brother the Gibechung leader, Günther, and his sister, Gutrune. Hagen is planning the return of the Ring to the Nibelungen, who are now Siegfried's slaves. His idea is to offer Gutrune to Siegfried and then having softened him up, get him to agree to penetrate the ring of fire and bring out Brünnhilde as wife for Günther. He means to accomplish this by administering a drug which will induce forgetfulness of Siegfried's past. While the draught of oblivion is an acceptable mechanism in mythic tales, like the love-draught in Tristan, it should be looked on with the same psychological realism. The drug is nothing other than the metaphor of our chosen forgetfulness in the face of our desires. Tristan and Isolde desire death since their love is impossible, and the love-potion simply allows them to express the passion they have before dying. Here, the drug is nothing less than Siegfried's encounter with the world of men. He is greeted as a hero, and offered the attractive Gibechung princess; in a world of swirling armies, celebrations and libations he is intoxicated with oath-taking ceremonies and royal hunts. He is the man of the moment and is having a wonderful time. The secret of Siegfried's behaviour from his entrance in the first act up until his betrayal must be one of enjoyment. In that sense he 'believes' the lies with which he will so shock Brünnhilde. He has become the adulterous husband lying to his wife, only now Fricka can do nothing, for the spear of the law is shattered.

Indeed, Hagen specifies exactly what the drug can do: as soon as he sees Gutrune in front of him he will forget that he had seen any other woman – a well known intoxication. Siegfried's horn announces his arrival on the river bank. The Gibechung leaders greet him effusively and he responds with warmth. He reveals to them under Hagen's probing that he carries the Tarnhelm but the Ring is still in Brünnhilde's possession. Gutrune hands him the drugged goblet, he drinks it in a toast to Brünnhilde and then takes in the beautiful presence of Gutrune, and with an impardonable pun on her name he grabs the unfortunate princess. Immediately they are plotting exactly what Hagen had hoped for, and

Siegfried is offering to present himself on the rock to Brünnhilde wearing the Tarnhelm and claiming her as a bride in Günther's name.

There follows the first oath-taking of the drama, intense and powerful in its emotion, the orchestra reminding us of what is in fact at stake. Siegfried and Günther swear an oath of blood brotherhood in a world where laws and contracts no longer count. Yet from this moment he has sealed his doom. As long as he was free he was safe, but now he has entered into a contract and lost the very spontaneity and power that was his. He has taken on the tragic responsibility for his destiny. The new allies set out immediately for the rock leaving Hagen alone to brood on the future. All he can think of or desire is the Ring.

On the rock Brünnhilde is visited by her sister Walküre, Waltraute. Brünnhilde, full of Siegfried, is scarcely interested in why she has come to visit her until with a sombre heart the visitor recounts what has become of their father, Wotan. Wotan now sits on his throne awaiting the end. He has refused Freia's apples, he has sent his ravens to circle the earth awaiting the news he longs for, and dreams of Brünnhilde returning the Ring to the Rhine Daughters. Waltraute begs her to do it.

She has come too late. For Brünnhilde the Ring only means one thing, the symbol of her love for Siegfried. She is finished with the gods and their world, she can barely remember Walhalla after her long sleep. Let it all fall in ruins – it means nothing to her. Horrified at this indifference, Waltraute rides off into the thunderstorm which brings with it the inexorable disaster. Siegfried, wearing the Tarnhelm presents himself as a claimant husband who has penetrated the fire. At last just as it seems that the Ring will finally be used, Siegfried snatches it from poor Brünnhilde's hand leaving her helpless. In a scene of near rape Siegfried takes her violently, but as she passes out in his arms, just for a moment, she looks into his eyes and recognises them. Declaring that he will spend the night with Notung between them to assure her chastity Siegfried follows the exhausted Brünnhilde into the cave.

Act Two opens with a scene of great intensity. Alberich appears to Hagen in a dream to confirm that he is intent on recovering the Ring. Subtly the balance of power shifts from Alberich to Hagen. Every time that Alberich invokes his paternal authority or speaks of them both in the plural Hagen stubbornly counters with reference to himself alone. He reminds him that he was bred to hatred and revenge, yet it becomes clear that that role is now enveloped in his own personality. When Alberich calls on him to swear to get the Ring he coolly replies:

| Mir selbst schwör' ich's; | I have sworn it to myself; |
| schweige die Sorge! | calm yourself |

Hagen's character is complete in the betrayal of his own father.

Siegfried returns to Gutrune and tells how he captured Brünnhilde for Günther. She questions him about their night together in the cave while he was disguised by the Tarnhelm but he assures her that they slept with the sword Notung between them. They go off to prepare for the arrival of the other two.

The next scene pulses with dramatic energy. Wagner has opened up the whole drama so that the people themselves, the Gibechung, now enter the story. Hagen calls on the people to make sacrifices to the gods and this is greeted with the virile enthusiasm of a people who clearly no longer believe in anything. Religion has been reduced to an excuse for public holidays. With the double wedding the Gibechung rule over the Rhinelands. The two couples arrive with all the ironic and bitter implications passionately commented upon by the music. It is when Brünnhilde raises her eyes and sees Siegfried that the first blow falls. She sees Siegfried with Gutrune, then she recognises the Ring on Siegfried's finger and the whole situation breaks in on her. Brünnhilde is overwhelmed as she realises she has been tricked and humiliated. Brünnhilde's claim that she is married to Siegfried is ignored and in her rage she transposes the claim, insisting that on the night before he had violated her while pretending to be Günther. Hagen, fully aware that his trap is springing just as he desired, offers his spear-point for Siegfried to swear his innocence. First Siegfried swears and then furiously Brünnhilde too swears that he may die for having broken his oath to her and perjured himself. His response is to bluster out of the situation and he hastily leads off Gutrune assuring the crowd who are in an uproar that the wild woman will calm down eventually.

Brünnhilde left alone with Hagen and Günther begins to try to comprehend what has happened. Hagen wins from Brünnhilde the secret he has been seeking. She confesses that when she magically protected his body from harm his back was left untouched by the spell since he was a brave warrior who never turned his back on a foe. Hagen assures her that Siegfried will pay with his life for the disgrace he has brought on her and on the Gibechung. Hagen confides in his step-brother that with Siegfried dead the Ring will once again be the Ring of the Nibelungen. Together they decide that he will be killed while out hunting the following day and that they will tell Gutrune he died in a hunting accident. While Brünnhilde and Günther together decide on the death of Siegfried, Hagen rejoices, in his enthusiasm acknowledging his father as the new Lord of the Ring.

The opening of Act Three with its meeting between Siegfried and the Rhine Daughters contains some of the most ravishing music in the Ring, made all the more poignant because the scene presents the hero with his last chance to save himself. The Rhine Daughters who have not forgotten how to flirt, almost cajole Siegfried into returning the Ring. Just as he is about to hand it to them they recount to him the curse on the Ring and warn him of the danger he is in, so that, in reaction, he declares he would never give the Ring back out of fear. The trap of destiny has sprung. It is because he is who he is and behaves as he does that his 'choice' is itself inevitable. Insisting he will not relinquish the Ring under threat he rejects their pleas. The Rhine Daughters more cogently point out his true position:

Eide schwur er –	He swore oaths
und achtet sie nicht!	and does not keep them!
Runen weiss er –	He knows secrets –
und rät sie nicht!	and does not heed them!

The next scene is the fatal hunting party. Siegfried entertains the huntsmen with his story of the slaying of the dragon and his converse with the Waldvogel. Hagen, ready to kill him, gives him another drug to restore his memory. As he tells how he reached Brünnhilde on the rock, loosened her armour and kissed her, Wotan's two ravens fly over the scene. Hagen asks if he can understand the ravens' cry and as Siegfried jumps to his feet to watch them fly overhead plunges his spear into Siegfried's back. Günther at the last moment tries to stop him but fails. Siegfried, who is mortally wounded, is illuminated by his memory of Brünnhilde. As he greets her he falls dead. There follows Siegfried's Trauermarsch which Newman described as 'too vast, too universal for association with mere human death, that seems rather to be such music as the spirit of the universe might hear when world crashes into world at the end of time.'

Hagen returns to the Gibechung's Hall exulting in his enemy's death. Günther, deeply shocked by what has happened tells his sister the truth. Hagen steps forward to claim the Ring from Siegfried's laid out body. Günther, insisting it is Brünnhilde's, tries to stop him. The brothers fall on each other and in an instant Günther is dead. As he tries to take the Ring from the dead man Siegfried's finger moves. At that moment Brünnhilde enters. She is no longer the betrayed wife or the romantic lover. She is ennobled by her grief and in complete command of the situation. She waves aside Gutrune's complaint without jealousy. It is no longer a question of marital infidelity.

Brünnhilde orders a funeral pyre for her husband's body. She confirms Siegfried's honour on the night of the Tarnhelm abduction, while admitting his deception with Gutrune. She has understood the whole pattern of events. All that has happened was necessary in order that she should gain wisdom. Now she understands. She orders the ravens to head for Walhalla. It is all over. Wotan's will is accomplished. With a serene tenderness she speaks to him:

Ruhe, ruhe, du Gott!	Rest, rest now, o god!

At last, fulfilling her own destiny she in turn takes up the Ring and places it on her finger. She orders the Rhine Daughters to take it from her ashes.

Das Feuer, das mich verbrennt,	The fire, in consuming me,
rein'ge vom Fluche den Ring!	Cleanses the Ring of its curse.

She tells the ravens, too, to call on Loge to prepare for the destruction of Walhalla, and hurtles her flaming torch onto the funeral pyre. Mounting Grane she leaps into the burning fire. The Rhine rises overflowing its banks and the music declares the presence of the Rhine Daughters who recover the ring and swim triumphantly holding it aloft. Hagen, horrified that he is about to lose the Ring dives into the water only to be dragged to his death by the Rhine Daughters. The Hall of the Gibech-ungs is destroyed. The mass of the people look up to the sky to see there, too, the destruction of the Hall of the Gods, Walhalla, where both gods and heroes sit awaiting the end. As the gods are engulfed in flames the curtain falls.

THE RING – ITS WORLD-VIEW

The myth is completed and the ancient tale has been told, its end leading back to its beginning in the form of a Ring. Nietzsche writing in 'Untimely Meditations' said: 'Der Ring des Nibelungen is a tremendous system of thought without the con-ceptual form of thought.'[46] Since Wagner thought 'mythically' his vision is not accessible to 'theo-retical man', yet it is in negation of theoretical man and in the need for a new kind of man that Nietzsche's own thinking is grounded. Nietzsche's own vision and thinking required a mythic framework to contain it, Zarathustra with his eagles and dwarfs and serpents lives in a world very recognisable to the Wagnerian. It only needed a philosopher to 'translate' the mythic vision not into theory but into deeply thought vision. This is what Nietzsche did with profundity and originality. Yet it is not a prosaic transposition of Wagner into philosophical meditation. From one point of view it was absolutely necessary for Nietzsche to break with Wagner if only to prevent the short circuiting of his thought. His nihilism demanded no allies, indeed even his own absence in his madness. He did not want to break with Wagner any more than he wanted to go mad. Yet he could not sustain the humiliation by his beloved Master any more than he could resist the spirochetes that destroyed his brain tissue. That is why it is more harmonious to consider Wagner as Nietzschean than the reverse. There are of course deep lacunae between the two. Nietzsche, while exalting the animal and erotic force of his Übermensch, still handled the score of Tristan with guilty gloves. His almost hysterical rejection of Parsifal while mistaken in its thesis was absolutely right from his position – it was not time for compassion! Least of all couched in what to him seemed christian language. Yet in the Ring there is no doubt but that we are swimming in the deepest springs of Nietzsche's inspiration and creative imagination.

Heidegger defined the five basic rubrics of Nietzsche's philosophy as being:

1. Nihilism.
2. Transvaluation of all values.
3. Will to power.
4. Eternal recurrence of the same.
5. Overman.[47]

Wagner's destruction of the gods embodies the first rubric, nihilism. From the beginning he intended the work to dramatise their end. This nihilism, like Nietzsche's, is not a negative force but rather is enormously exhilarating. Wotan's end is not tragic for its gift is the future. In 'Thus Spoke Zarathustra' it says:

'To redeem the past and to transform every it-was into an I-wanted-it-thus! – that alone do I call redemption.'[48]

It is this nihilism that is the necessary prelude to the transvaluation of all values. As Bakunin in the social sphere observed, the new society could not be built until the old had been destroyed. It is Brünnhilde's act which not only sweeps away the old order but heralds a new, for Brünnhilde has brought into events a completely new principle. The rule of exterior state powers and contracts is gone. In its place has come Siegfried's revitalising spontaneity and innocence. It in turn goes down before the sheer cynicism of politics and his own amoral response to sexuality. The first has cruelly punished Brünnhilde and the second has betrayed her. Yet in these experiences she comes to understand that the two men she loved could not do anything else within their limits. Her suffering bursts the bonds of her own limitations – the rejected daughter and the abandoned wife – and she enters the sphere of politics, but with a new weapon. From Wotan she has learned to will the end, and from Siegfried to be, supremely, herself. To these she brings her own newfound compassion. It is this that transforms her end from a primitive suttee into an act of liberation.

Thus the Götterdämmerung leads directly to a confirmation of renewal. Heidegger says: 'With nihilism – that is to say, with the revaluation of all prior values among beings as will to power and in the light of the eternal recurrence of the same – it becomes necessary to posit a new essence of man.'[49] Here Heidegger is demonstrating the relatedness of Nietzsche's five principles. Defining 'will to power' he says: 'What is will to power? It is "the innermost essence of Being" (WM 693). That is to say, will to power is the basic character of beings as such. The essence of will to power can therefore be examined and thought only with regard to beings as such; that is, metaphysically.' He finds Nietzsche's definition in Zarathustra – 'In the section "On Self-Overcoming" Nietzsche says: Where I found the living, there I found will to power, and even in the will of those who serve I found the will to be master.'[50]

It is significant that the element in Schopenhauer which Wagner felt obliged to reject was that pessimism which was inescapably bound to his doctrine of the will and it is the same element which Nietzsche demolishes with his transformation of the will into will-to-power. A rigid and static edifice is turned into a dynamic motor force. Zarathustra's mountain and Brünnhilde's are not dissimilar, in that both descend to announce the destruction of the gods, and that meant to both their creators the end of the judaeo-christian hegemony both metaphysically and politically.

Will to power throughout the cycle has been demonstrated by the quest and capture of the Ring. Relentlessly it has been sought and as inevitably brought destruction on its owners. The will to power as the force of existence and as the catalyst of transvaluation has also manifested itself in the opposing force, the Overman who must break the bondage of the Ring's inhibiting curse. Since in the end it withholds its own power, it must be opposed and overthrown to allow will to power to operate anew. Politically translated, usury does not in the end enrich, but impoverishes, until the whole world is endebted. Once the money-flow has become the dominant force in society then men cease to be. Only a new man will have the power to decide TO DO WITHOUT THE INTEREST CYCLE AND ITS LEGENDARY POWER, and thus free mankind from the bondage of usury, and that is exactly what Brünnhilde does in the myth – she decides that she simply does not want the Ring. As Wagner wrote: 'We will recognise that human society is sustained, not by the supposed operation of money, but by that of its members.'[51]

Will to power manifests itself in political and psychological language throughout the saga, beginning with the slave Nibelung choosing power when denied erotic distraction, and ending with Brünnhilde choosing freedom after being erotically betrayed. It reaches its Schopenhauerian peak in Wotan's acceptance of the necessary, but it achieves its Nietzschean depassement in Brünnhilde's liberating act which restores existence to its basic primal conditions – for will to power to express itself anew.

On the face of it this points to a hindu sense of cyclic history. In Zarathustra, Nietzsche's dwarf (Alberich?) wrongly interprets the doctrine of the eternal return of the same as meaning that time is circular. In 'Thus Spoke Zarathustra' Nietzsche's hero declares: 'I, Zarathustra, the advocate of life, the advocate of suffering, the advocate of the circle – I call you, my most abysmal thought. Ah! You are coming – I hear you! My abyss SPEAKS, I have turned my ultimate depth into the light.'[52]

Heidegger comments: '...we have learned no longer to think nihilism "nihilistically" as complete dissolution into vacuous nothingness. Neither, then, can valuelessness or aimlessness any longer signify a lack or mere vacuity and absence. These nihilistic epithets touching beings as a whole mean something affirmative that occurs essentially; that is, they mean the WAY IN WHICH the whole of beings comes to presence. The metaphysical expression for this is the eternal return of the same.'[53]

Nietzsche's insistence on the world having no goal and no 'total value' is affirmative and liberating. Heidegger comments:

'If being as such is will to power and thus eternal Becoming, and if will to power demands endlessness and excludes endless

progress towards an end in itself; if at the same time the eternal Becoming of will to power is delimited in its possible configurations and constructs of domination, because it cannot be new unto infinity; then being as a whole as will to power must permit the same to recur and must be an eternal return of the same. This 'circuit' embodies the 'primal law' of beings as a whole, if being as such is will to power.
'Eternal return of the same is the way in which the impermanent (that which becomes) as such comes to presence; it comes to presence in the highest form of permanence (in circling), with the sole determination of securing its possibility to be empowered.'[54]

Heidegger's reflections on this difficult subject merit study for they come to the heart of the matter. He explains: 'That which is to come is precisely a matter of decision, since the ring is not closed in some remote infinity but possesses its unbroken enclosure in the Moment, as the centre of the striving; what recurs – if it is to recur – is decided by the Moment and by the force with which the Moment can cope with whatever in it is repelled by such striving. That is what is peculiar to, and hardest to bear in, the doctrine of eternal return – to wit, that eternity IS in the Moment, that the Moment is not the fleeting "now", not an instant of time whizzing by a spectator, but the collision of future and past. Here the Moment comes to itself. It determines how everything recurs.'[55]

Of course, all this implies that as Heidegger admits, 'Nietzsche himself knew that his "most abysmal thought" remains a riddle.'[56] Yet it is this dimension of the Ring that obsesses us more and more as we become involved in it. Immediately, we grasp that a ring itself is the perfect metaphor for the eternal return of the same and is indeed used by Nietzsche to allow him to talk about it. In Wagner's myth the Ring is held in the depths of the Rhine – where it 'belongs' – but then, once will to power moves, it transmutes into specificity, choices, and these choices must be will to power. The Ring is 'forged' by the Nibelungen. It is given form where before it was potential. Mythic existence where all meanings are present yet held in suspension gives way to historic existence where they become actualised in the very goals which existence cannot sustain thus guaranteeing suffering. This is the narrative of the Ring saga. It is this that is glimpsed by Brünnhilde when her suffering is illuminated by her compassion, or we could say when her neurosis is dispelled by her action. Thus the motive revealed by Sieglinde which announces Brünnhilde's secret: 'O hehrstes Wunder! Herrlichste Maid!' is the result of her free action to save the unborn Siegfried. It is this free act which at the end, in the moment of total destruction of a whole society is revealed to be the underlying truth, that surfaces in the glorious music as it sweeps over the ruins of a world bathing them in light and serenity. The 'riddle' of philosophy becomes the tremendous musical statement of the Ring and with its syntax of motivic units is able to speak, as Wagner had insisted it could, what could not be spoken.

The steps to create the Übermensch are Wotan's achievement. This is his 'great thought' referred to in Rheingold. The sword, Notung is not enough, for Notung itself is 'need' and so is part of the apparatus of necessities. The required instrument is the free being. Siegmund, the hero sires Siegfried, and he wins as his bride, Brünnhilde, daughter of heaven and earth, Wotan and Erda. Siegmund is the first bridge to the Overman. He, however, is based on need (Notung) and as Fricka realises, is therefore inauthentic. Siegfried is the free hero, spontaneous animality, the very fundamental element which Nietzsche insisted as the truth of the Overman. Yet he becomes a victim of his own innocence and sexual force. Brünnhilde at the very end is able to bring about the destruction of the gods and achieve the desired new beginning.

> Heidegger: 'Thus Zarathustra, who teaches the Overman, concludes the first part of his teaching with the words: "DEAD ARE ALL GODS: NOW WE WILL THAT OVER-MAN LIVE – at some great midday let this be our ultimate will! – " At the time of the most luminous brightness, when beings as a whole show themselves as eternal recurrence of the same, the will must will the Overman; for only within the prospect of the Overman is the thought of the eternal return of the same to be borne. The will that wills here is not a yearning and striving, but will to power. The "we" who are willing in it are those who have experienced the basic character of beings as will to power, those who know that at its zenith will to power itself wills its own essence and thus is concordant with beings as a whole.'[57]

And so, as the exultant music reverberating and descending into radiant peace that is the end of Götterdämmerung resolves itself into its final chords, the tremendous illumination and confirm-ation which we experience in this astonishing scene of absolute destruction and devastation, is that now, and only now has the way been cleared for the emergence of the Overman. The final scene is described by Wagner in these words: 'From the ruins of the fallen hall, the men and women, IN GREAT AGITATION, watch the growing fire-light in the heavens. When this reaches its greatest brightness, the hall of Walhalla is seen, in which gods and heroes sit assembled, just as Waltraute described them in the first act. Bright flames seize on the hall of the gods. When the gods are entirely hidden by the flames, the curtain falls.' With Wagner's magisterial dramatic sense 'we' are represented on the stage viewing the downfall of the gods in the utmost dismay, for it has followed, do not forget, the destruction of 'our' human state-system. It is left to the music to take us out beyond the scene of absolute annihilation to breathe the new freedom – now that the Overman can emerge at last!

> Heidegger: 'Yet whence arises the urgent cry for the Overman? Why is prior humanity no longer enough? Because Nietzsche recognises the historic moment in which man takes it on himself to assume dominion over the earth as a whole. Nietzsche is the first thinker to pose the decisive question concerning the phase of world history that is

emerging only now, the first to think the question through in its metaphysical implications. The question asks: Is man, in his essence as man heretofore, prepared to assume dominion over the earth? If not, what must happen with prior humanity in order that it may 'subjugate' the earth and thus fulfil the prophecy of an old testament? Must not prior man be conducted beyond himself, OVER his prior self, in order to meet this challenge? If so, then the "Over-man", correctly thought, cannot be the product of an unbridled and degenerate fantasy that is plunging headlong into the void. We can just as little uncover the nature of Overman historically by virtue of an analysis of the modern age. We dare not seek the essential figure of Overman in those personalities who, as major functionaries of a shallow, misguided will to power, are swept to the pinnacles of that will's sundry organisational forms. Of course, one thing ought to be clear to us immediately: this thinking that pursues the figure of a teacher who teaches the Over-man involves us, involves Europe, involves the earth as a whole – not merely today, but especially tomorrow.'[58]

And can it be said that the stern teacher of the Overman carries the same message as Brünnhilde leaping into the flames, liberated by love? Heidegger's response to this is simple: 'As the teacher of eternal recurrence, Zarathustra teaches the Overman. According to an unpublished note (XIV, 276), a refrain accompanies the latter doctrine: "Refrain: LOVE ALONE WILL MAKE IT RIGHT" – (the creative love that FORGETS itself in its works).'[59]

Let us give the Master the last word:

> 'A PERFORMANCE is something I can conceive of only AFTER THE REVOLUTION; only the Revolution can offer me the artists and listeners I need. The coming Revolution must necessarily put an end to this whole THEATRICAL BUSINESS of ours: they must all perish, and will certainly do so, it is inevitable. Out of the ruins I shall summon together what I need: I shall THEN find what I require. I shall put up a theatre on the Rhine and send out invitations to a great dramatic festival: after a year's preparations I shall perform my entire work within the space of FOUR DAYS: WITH IT I shall then make clear to the men of the Revolution the MEANING of that Revolution,

in its noblest sense. THIS AUDIENCE will understand me: present-day audiences cannot.'[60]

4

WAGNER AND GERMANY

Wagner's dedication of the Ring declared: 'Composed with confidence in the German spirit.' It is not possible to come to grips with the Wagnerian phenomenon without a view of his 'Germanness'. Either this is something to be abhorred or it is a vital aspect of the composer's creativity. Does it exclude us from him or confirm him to us? His whole work contains an astonishing homogeneity, it is like one great epic. Viewed as a psychological exploration or as a mythic oeuvre, it is seen to be a profound statement on the human condition. Yet from the beginning it is supremely 'German'. The libretti – or dramas, if you prefer – are not only written in German but they also claim to be poems in their own right. As literature they are of varying quality, although it should be added that they do not stick to only one form.

The Ring is written basically in the ancient alliterative verse-form of stabreim. Tristan abandons grammatical structure in the most radical way and while strange on the page it proves ideal for the quite amazing role it has within its musical framework. Meistersinger is probably the only work which can stand on its own as a quite pleasing literary achievement. Of course, the truth is they are not complete until they become music. Yet in these texts can be discerned how overtly and passionately Wagner was German.

Wagner's scholarship has now been thoroughly researched and the old idea that somehow he was a simple composer with intellectual 'pretensions' duly swept away. The erudition of the man is impressive even in his epoch, and his library remains a part of our European heritage. It was after Tannhäuser that he began to study Gervinus' 'Geschichte der poetischen Nationalliteratur der Deutschen' and Jakob Grimm's massive 'Deutsche Mythologie'. And so from Tannhäuser up to Parsifal, with the exception of the Celtic Tristan which nevertheless had its rich German source in Gottfried von Strassburg's thirteenth century version, Wagner never left the 'world' of Germany.

The unity of the underlying psychological mapping in his life's work is matched by an imaginary Germany in which the music-dramas take place, for even when the location is not geographically Germany it always is at the mythic level. Biographism only obscures an understanding of Wagner which is perhaps why from Newman to Gregor-Dellin the reader is left with the uncomfortable sensation that the more one knows of Wagner's life the more obscured become the works. In a way this is not surprising, for Wagner was, after all, a man living his time, a nineteenth century composer trying to survive, let alone write a completely new kind of music-drama while the whole world around him seemed to be in continual upheaval. One trouble with Wagner is that he is so vast in his creativity and so ahead of his time not just aesthetically but imaginatively that when he – and this is the biographical zone – suddenly reveals himself over a contemporary issue to be utterly banal or depressingly wrong we feel betrayed. It is not fair to expect him loftily to refuse the handouts of the mad Ludwig, how fortunate for him and for us that he should have come upon so unusual a benefactor. At the end of the nineteenth century one had to be profoundly insane and very rich to grasp that Wagner was going to shake the world. There was not some other Ludwig in some other Venusberg waiting further up the Rhine if he failed to provide the necessary support. Wagner was well aware of this, and in the end his meddling in court affairs is a sign of his reckless search for at least a gesture of independence, where in fact he had none.

Wagner's Germany was for him, as for his enlightened contemporaries, a matter of almost unbearable contradiction. It was in the centre of the European upheaval and subversion of traditional christian values, it was experiencing the impact of a massive influx of jewish refugees from Poland and Russia, it was witnessing the end of the principalities – and the decadence of Ludwig's Bavaria is a sign of that end – and it was witnessing the Bismarckian solution of the unified Second Reich.

There was not really any way Wagner could have a clear politique – no one else had, and those who did were Bismarckian, a position the composer could never be completely happy with, believing as he did in the free individual and the abolition of the state. Thus, biographically we find him changing ground again and again. What has to be understood is that the ground itself was changing under him all during his lifetime.

While Wagner among his contemporaries was both a patriotic German, a dangerous and black-listed revolutionary, and the protege of a mad homosexual monarch, he was also the composer of a quite new kind of music which to the credit of the educated public of the time was recognised and confirmed during his own life. In the end it should be noted that Ludwig did very well for a madman. He made possible the great masterworks of Richard Wagner for the whole world, and for his native Bavaria by building his fabled castles he laid the foundations for the state's future tourist industry. At the end of Wagner's life, with the achievement of Bayreuth, the composer himself became a part of 'Germanness'. He came to stand for that very essence of what was German which he had so failed to define in his theoretical writings let alone his private letters. Both Nietzsche and Wagner moved between excoriating and poeticising the German spirit, both could be said to have contradicted themselves on the subject. Yet the basic viewpoint is very similar through the Teutonic dust which seemed to cloud the subject.

Wagner's Germany was a mountain view, a Hölderlin vision of a spiritual domain. It was the 'nation' of Goethe's Faust, and his beloved Mozart's Die Zauberflöte, and quintessentially of Beethoven's Ninth Symphony. This meant that his

'Germany' was a light for mankind and a promise of freedom – a freedom which had not been realised in the Europe of his day. He had warned in his youth, in Lohengrin, of the danger to this Germany from the hordes from the east. He warned in his maturity of the spiritual danger from the west. He warned in Parsifal of the inner danger from the denial of compassion. History proved him – in this vision – correct on all three matters. The east took half of the land and plunged it into political slavery, the west invaded with its destruction of culture through the exaltation of market-values, after the Third Reich which doctrinally rejected compassion had already failed to create the new Germany. From 1939 Adolf Hitler, an erudite Wagnerian, forbade the performance of Parsifal. Did it ever occur to him that since he denied the Master's final guidance, he would be destined to live out the apocalyptic end of that first vision in Rienzi, where the populist hero was doomed to a tower of fire, rejected by the same people he had raised up from degradation to greatness?

Neither the Second nor the Third Reich could claim Wagner, nor, for that matter the bankers' new united Germany. Each, in its way would have been appalling to him. The longed-for breaking of the chains of men had never happened, nor was it going to in the hundred years after his death.

Indeed, European man is radically less free in today's so-called democracies than he had been in the Third Reich. Police today have more far-reaching powers and legislative support for arbitrary arrest than ever in history, and the computerising of citizens' records assures their all but helpless political condition, to say nothing of the danger in which they may lie from techno-logised torture.

Wagner wrote: 'I carry my Germany around within me.'[61] His Germany – that realm that envisioned and embodied these great hymns to the human spirit and its freedom by Goethe, Mozart and Beethoven – has not yet become a political reality. The profound tragedy of today is that the modern German, for the crudest and most cynical reasons of political manipulation has been indoctrinated almost totally to be ashamed of 'that' Germany. In order that the very usurocracy which Wagner dreaded, might dominate world markets, it was considered absolutely necessary to prevent the Wagnerian vision being understood by modern people. Goethe they could hand over to the universities, soon his existential realism would be blurred in the language of structuralism and semiotics. Mozart, to Wagner 'the greatest and most divine genius,'[62] was to be psycho-analysed as a copraphiliac punk. Beethoven's towering hymn to freedom could be made the 'european' monetarist national anthem. Wagner was dangerous. He had been when alive, and now that usury had evolved into a world system and its institutions and method had successfully endebted the whole world rendering all state power obedient to it, he was more dangerous than ever.

Discrediting Wagner biographically worked neither in books nor on television. He was simply too great to be silenced. The silence, after 1945, lasted into the '50s. Since it was clear that people were simply going to insist on hearing his work again on stage the first concession was made. It should be remembered that the destruction of both Wahnfried and the Festival Theatre at Bayreuth had been planned and even reconsidered. The American soldiers urinating on Wagner's grave and the humiliation of the Wagner family were forgotten. What emerged was a Wagner in vacuo. His works were to be presented in limbo. No ancient Germany, no Rhine, no Nürnberg, nothing, nowhere. To give these post-war Bayreuth presentations some semblance of intellectual re-spect it was declared that they were 'psychological' readings of the works, so in place of the German Wagner the world was given the Jungian Wagner, trapped in the Swiss cuckoo-clock of the anima-animus mechanism. This also allowed a retroactive rejection of 'the Bayreuth tradition' and Cosima's dictatorial protection of the early naturalistic production style. So, in turn, with that went all serious thinking about Wagner as an intellectual with something to say about the modern world. In the process, what the Wagner family, from Cosima, through Winifred, to the grandsons, had done was keep Wagner presentation alive, through two wars and two Reichs and beyond. Alas, after these heroic struggles they now seem bent on its betrayal.

In all of this, the history of Wagner production, what emerges is the enormous difficulty there has been in letting the public reach the Wagnerian world. He has not been presented so much as blocked. Once reason began to enter even a little into public discourse it became necessary to reassess the great German, but, and this is one of the most disturbing sociological facts of our culture, not before the German people had been by and large made to feel as if liking Wagner was something to be ashamed of – and that meant, by extension – that inner Germany of which Wagner had spoken, the realm of Goethe's Faust, Mozart and Beethoven. Where once it had been the Germans who had gone crazy over Wagner now the world was to be permitted to enthuse – under strict ideological conditions – but to the Germans it could no longer be permitted.

It is because Wagner is supremely German, grounded and immersed in his own history and mythic past, caught up in his own tumultuous present with its reactionaries and its revolutionaries, and so inspired by a Germany to come that will at some point in time burst out into that very freedom so beloved of the mighty Beethoven and the ecstatic Mozart, so sure that men could be educated like Wilhelm Meister to be sound human beings, no danger to themselves or other people, it is for these matters that we all recognise him for the universal spirit his musical works declare him to be.

5

WAGNER AND RELIGION

The deepest realm of Wagner's Germanness was his spirituality. His knowledge of the truth of divine illumination, which is the central experience of his dramas, convinced him of the inauthenticity of judaism and christianity. On January 31st, 1883, a few days before his death, he was writing of the church as 'a terrible warning example'.[63] It had failed miserably. On this he was uncompromising. Writing to Hans von Wolzogen in 1880 he spoke of 'the future meaning and significance... of the historically intelligible figure of Jesus of Nazareth...

who must first be cleansed and redeemed of the distortion that has been caused by Alexandrine, Judaic and Roman despotism.'[64] A 'future' view of Jesus can only be one which, while confirming his sublime radiance and compassion, recognises him as a man and not a being somehow enmeshed in a complex relationship with creation and its redemption, whatever that might be. About the christian system, both catholic and protestant, he was in no doubt: 'Nevertheless, although we are merciless in abandoning the Church and the priesthood and indeed the whole historical phenomenon of christianity, our friends must always know that we do so for the sake of that same Christ... so that... we can take him with us into those terrible times which may very well follow the necessary destruction of all that at present exists.'[65]

With the flowering of Tannhäuser's staff, Wagner had in those early days moved out from the shadow of the Church's claimed hegemony of spirituality. In terms of political power Wagner was in no doubt. The great edifice of the Ring is throbbing with a sense of destiny and meaning. Religion as a formal structure is a matter of oath-taking in the name of the distant gods. The vibrant sense of providential energy is expressed in the encounter both with nature and with solitude. Wagner as well as Nietzsche celebrated the end of the judaeo-christian ethos both morally and politically, the latter by announcing the death of 'their' god, and the former by projecting a new religion, undefined, into the future, which preserved the transcendental force of compassion over human affairs. That its contours were not so hidden we are beginning to understand.

It is an intriguing footnote to the epoch in which religion gave way to its secularised decadent forms which recounts the tale of Freud and the Ring. Seeking a way to assure that this 'power' of psycho-analysis should remain strictly under the priesthood of Freud and his acolytes, one of his initiates proposed to him that each practising psycho-analyst should be given a Ring engraved with Freud's signature as proof of membership to the magic circle. Only wearers of the Ring would be entitled to wield its power through the practice of psycho-analysis. Freud was enormously excited at this idea and agreed, then later had second thoughts, perhaps in a lucid moment while free of his cocaine addiction.

Just as the Ring places man in a position of being at the last liberated from dependence on transcendental framing, so Tristan presents man's encounter with the erotic drive in all its eruptive power. In Tristan, God is not mentioned. All we are faced with is the titanic encounter of two people of vast psychic power hurtling themselves against the limits of their own selfhood and savagely tearing down its final barrier in order that the one should melt into the other, vividly aware that if each does it the result will be mutual annihilation. They achieve their desire against all the attempts of the outside world to separate them and even let them live. Tristan tears off his bandages in a delirium of self-destruction which is worthwhile because Isolde is there to see it, and she sinks exhausted to the point of death over his body, for now she is free to die.

This tumultuous and passionate encounter, Wagner's 'perfect work', reaches its climax in what is called Isolde's Verklärung, that is, Transfiguration. It is not a tragedy. The end is the triumph of the so-called lovers. Yet it is clear from the astonishing images and metaphors of the text that they do not in any real way want each other and the famous union of the lovers, popularly and most incorrectly named the love-duet, while it is swooningly sensual cannot be called erotic in the sense that it does not sexually arouse us. We are quite aware that its content is undisguisedly sexual. Here, as Michael Tanner brilliantly points out, we are in that modern world where sexuality is recognised to be a vital spiritual force, a theme whose spokesman was the still little understood D. H. Lawrence.

The 'love-duet' is not coitus interruptus nor is it the onset of schizophrenia as some recent stage directors have suggested. The whole procedure of the drama is the unfolding of the human spirit's exploration and eventual obliteration of the self. The genius of Wagner lay in his refusal, or incapacity, to hide the sexual identity of the spiritual faculty. As the Sufis say, 'You cannot love if you have not been in love.' Not just sexuality itself, but life is metaphoric. More than that, music is the language of this cross-over from the sign to the signified, as Wagner put it 'to express the inexpressible'. At the end of Tristan it is not an orgasm we experience or desire, it is transfiguration. The obliteration of the selfhood of both Tristan and Isolde is encompassed by the listener. It is metaphor for us of that genuine and authentic spiritual experience which is not transcendence but annihilation.

Shaykh al-'Alawi of Algeria in his Diwan sings of it, too:

> 'She took me. She possessed me.
> She made me withdraw in her meaning.
> Until I thought that she was me and
> that my spirit was her ransom.
> She changed me. She developed me.

She brought me up to her height.
She gathered me. She isolated me.
She named me with her name.
She slew me. She tore me to shreds.
She dyed me with her blood.
After my death, she brought me to life.
My star shone in her sky.
Where is my spirit? Where is my body?
Where is self and its passion?'

The natural religion (fitra) has reached its innermost essence in contemplation of annihilating love (sufism). Wagner's work is not a deliberate and planned unified work as the early Bayreuthians suggested, yet it is one whole symphonic statement raising the inevitable contradictions of themes which must be wrestled with and resolved. Wagner had no doubt about the elimination of the false priesthood religions of judaism and christianity. His Ring triumphantly declares the death of the gods, and that meant the same as it did for Nietzsche, the end of the judaeo-christian moral tyranny. Wagner's journey, however, could not stop there. He had to resolve the apparent dichotomy that the old religion had set up between spirituality and sexuality. In Tristan he found the language and the meaning. There remained one last testament which would permit him to sum up these subjects so dear to his life and so important to him. Appropriately, the author of its legend had witnessed Tannhäuser's pilgrimage towards the truth, in Wagner's opera. Wolfram von Eschenbach's Middle High German poem of Parsifal was to end up, transformed as only Wagner knew how, into the first vision of a new religion. So uncompromisingly 'religious' was the work, and so uncomfortably post-judaeo-christian, that many of Wagner's contemporaries mistook his final work for a last arrogant attempt to create his own brand of religion, woven out of art itself. This was not the case, any more than he intended Tristan to be a love story. Parsifal was for Wagner not only his farewell, but his summing up, and not only his summing up for he could never bear to be finished, revolutionary that he was, but also his opening to the future. It was a vision. All his gazing and meditating on the past was his reaching into the future.

In our previous reflections on Parsifal we moved our perspective from the traditional view that it was a pseudo-christian compromise to the more tenable idea that it at least was not a piece of christian embroidery, but rather a drama of existential transformation. To terminate our Wagnerian journey let us examine Parsifal again, bearing in mind that it is also, according to its creator, a postscript to the Ring, and its hero Parsifal the fulfilment of what was thwarted in the tragic destruction of Siegfried.

Up until now however we have looked at these works as speaking their subject matter not only in a coherent way but in a way consciously confirmed by the composer. Here we will take the liberty of making an interpretation, but one based on all that had gone before and a viewpoint remarkably sustained by internal evidence and Wagner's own tastes. It would be patently false, and a worthless task, to suggest that what is here analysed was what Wagner 'meant'. It does not mean that in a new reading of the work we cannot perceive what is implied and what is harmonious with that underlying orientation. What we propose is clearly much more apposite than viewing it as a William Morris piece of medievalism, and certainly nearer the mark than one recent presentation which located the drama around Wagner's upper lip overlooking his nostrils.

Right at the beginning we are given three pieces of information. Monsalvat, the domain of the Grail, is like the northern mountains of Gothic Spain. Klingsor's castle lies on the southern mountains of Gothic Spain. Klingsor's castle lies on the southern side of the mountains 'which looks towards Moorish Spain'. The Grail Knights' uniform resembles that of the Templars, however instead of the red cross on their cloaks there is emblazoned a white dove. Thus, the action of Parsifal is located on the frontier of Christianity, on its edge, facing Islamic Spain.

The christian Grail community is sick. Trapped in the cult of atonement, blood sacrifice and guilt they wither away, men without women, monks without illumination. It is 'the Waste Land' of the christian dilemma, and at its heart the deluding and destroying notion that sexuality is in itself unclean. Their vitality and manliness which is symbolised by the Spear has been stolen by Klingsor when he trapped Amfortas, the Grail King in his magic garden of sexual delights. Wounded by the Spear, Amfortas now pines away ashamed, rejecting his role as the one who must reveal the Grail to its initiates. His aged father, dying, lingers on in the hope of it being revealed again. Into this gloomy and disastrous realm stumbles the innocent fool, Parsifal. Kept from war by his mother he knows no arms except a bow and arrow he uses for hunting. He shoots a swan, and it is this action which brings him before Gurnemanz, ensnaring him in the anguished problems of the Grailists. Parsifal's balsam brought by Kundry is Arabian, the country's nearness is felt, present, in the events. The end of the christian world is imminent. The whole of the first act is the annunciation of the saving hero who will renew the Grail, the one who has been made wise by compassion.

Act Two takes place in Klingsor's Magic Castle. At its opening Klingsor sits before 'a metal mirror' – a masonic artefact – surrounded by 'magical and necromantic apparatus'. Just as Act One was the domain of a dying christianity so Act Two is the last enclave of a doomed Kabbalistic judaism. Where, in the christian world, man is the victim of sexual guilt and unnatural celibacy, in the jewish world woman is the victim. Kundry, the beautiful jewess, is the helpless slave of Klingsor, the necromantic rabbi. He rules by curses in the talmudic tradition – for his is not the judaism of Moses with its legality and justice, but a perverted religion that sets its followers apart from the rest of mankind which can only be tolerated once it is totally controlled. Klingsor holds the band of young ex-Grailists in captivity by enslaving them to their sexual appetites with the drugged and enchanting Flower Maidens who sing and dance to lure their victims to distraction from the real world. What had at first seemed medieval legend, becomes on closer examination more relevant to the modern world which has witnessed a generation of Flower Children enchant the world to the dictates of its Klingsors while the christian civilisation stood by, bereft of moral authority, exhausted by wars, watching the world's wealth being taken out of its hands. Klingsor himself does not fight but gets the drugged christian warriors to do his fighting for him. He had wanted to be one of them and accepted by them but they had despised him – all his actions since have been motivated by revenge and dynamised by curses. His real desire is that all the christian knights should mutually destroy each other. To obey the rules of celibacy he had even castrated himself, and now openly opposed to the christians can never forgive them. He is incapable of love, as he had been incapable of being loved. All that remains is for him to accomplish his revenge by possessing the Grail itself and thus conquer the christian world utterly.

The Flower Children, singing of peace and love, try to draw Parsifal into their psychedelic garden but Kundry's appearance terrifies them and they vanish. Kundry – Wagner's brilliant study in schizophrenia – while longing to be saved from her torment by Parsifal cannot resist obeying her orders from Klingsor and attempting to seduce him, knowing that to succeed will mean losing her chance of being healed. The passionate kiss Parsifal receives shocks him – not into arousal of sexual passion but into a sudden raw awareness of Amfortas' torment. Critics have been so impressed by the deep psychological binding of Kundry's sexuality with the tapping in Parsifal of the memory of his mother's love that they fail to note the other strand of the story. Parsifal's awakening is highly significant for the Grail Brotherhood. What happens is that when he is kissed by Kundry he suddenly understands the trap – he has dredged out of his own being the very cause of the christians' failure to rule, and the reason for the power of the Hollywood dream factory, that is, Klingsor's Magic Garden, over their culture and life.

When he is kissed he cries out:

Amfortas!	Amfortas!
Die Wunde! – Die Wunde!	The wound! The wound!
Sie brennt in meinem Herzen!	It burns in my heart!
O! Klage! Klage!	O! Torment! Torment!
aus tiefstem Herzem	the anguished cry
schreit sie mir auf.	pierces my heart.
O! O! Elender!	O! Miserable piteous man.
Jammervollster!	
Die Wunde seh ich bluten,	The Wound that I saw
nun blutet sie in mir!	bleeding now bleeds in me!

By bonding the natural sexual impulse of man for woman to the memory of love for the mother a seal of guilt is set on the heart of the man. Once this is known he can be ruled since he no longer trusts his intrinsic self. This is the psycho-analytical system – this is what Nietzsche termed ressentiment, the pact between the guilty christian and the punishing rabbi. Parsifal cries out:

Wie alles schauert, bebt und zuckt in sündigem Verlangen!	How all things tremble, quiver and shake in sinful, guilty yearning!

Parsifal has heard Jesus in his heart call on him to save the christian from this trap. As yet he does not see the way, but now he understands. Kundry's last plea to Parsifal to redeem her is answered openly. She will be granted both love and redemption if she takes him to Amfortas. At that moment – in Act Two – Parsifal declares the end of the guilt transaction of the Eucharist as a magical procedure to assure redemption from guilt. The end of the Eucharist is the end of Pauline (jewish) christianity and the way is open to pure religion. Kundry takes refuge in the ultimate retreat of her talmudic magic by calling a curse upon him – that he, like her, should wander forever, homeless. Parsifal's capture of the Spear is the symbolic confirmation of his resolve to fight and his recovery of the lost virility that had been held ransom by Klingsor's magical ressentiment. The end of Act Two declares an end not only to Kabbalistic judaism but to the fatal pact between judaism and christianity which is itself the root of usury.

Act Three takes place years later. Gurnemanz is now old and grey. The Grail Community is doom-laden, lingering, waiting for an end to their desolation. The once heroic knights are now reduced to digging for roots to survive. Into this misery strides the new Parsifal. The boy with his bow and arrow has become a man and a warrior. He enters, superbly accoutred in black armour, the image of his as yet unborn son Lohengrin, who will one day appear to the Germans to set them on the path to future freedom. The still pacifist christians require that he remove his armour, which courteously he does. His path has taken him to many lands and he has fought many battles. Now free of the curse on him he has found his way back to Monsalvat in order to liberate its inhabitants and institute the new religion. At first Parsifal finds himself still held back by the lingering effects of ressentiment but Gurnemanz steps in to activate the hero into taking on his role as their saviour.

It is here that everything becomes transformed. Not just nature, and not just the central protagonists, but the very rites of the dead religion. Wagner had written: 'God will give us light to find the right law.'[66] In Parsifal, at least in visionary terms, he points the way. In October of 1852 he had declared, speaking of Hafiz, the great Persian Sufi (Parsi-fool?):

'He is the greatest and sublimest philosopher; so certainly and irrefutably no one ever yet understood the world's secret.'[67] Islam was not an alien religion, since Ibn Rushd, indeed, it had been at the core of European civilisation. It was the primal religion, prior to rabbinical and priestly corruptions. It was the final religion which was for all mankind, designed to replace the state and confer freedom on men – Wagner's longed-for 'one religion and no state'.[45]

What happens next is the transformation of all the christian rites into their Islamic equivalent. Firstly Parsifal declares himself King. Islam being law is founded on leadership. He bathes himself in water – the act of baptism is transformed into the act of wudhu' or ritual purification by water before prayer. Parsifal, following Qur'anic instruction, bathes his face and head, arms and feet. The act is completed by an anointing which in turn is the perfuming of the muslim. The 'Good' Friday of the calendar becomes the Friday instituted as the day of public worship, for the magical act of blood-sacrifice is abolished and what remains to be celebrated is the blessing of the compassionate community. Holy blood is no longer elevated thus the vision of the Grail as 'Cup' is no longer required. Parsifal heals Amfortas of his wound – which was guilt itself, or if you like, the christian aberration. Kundry too is saved. She enters the christian community, for she cannot reach the pure religion until she has made her peace with them and become one of them, which means the end of separatist judaism. Then, and only then Parsifal takes up his final duty.

Nicht soll er mehr verschlossen sein:	No more shall it be hidden:
Enthüllet den Gral, öffnet den Schrein!	Uncover the Grail, open the shrine!

It is the end of the initiative communicant church, and thus the end of the initiating excommunicating priest. Religion is for all mankind without intermediary or meta-history or race-magic. The Grail-veil can be made to reveal its true identity.

In a long and complicated essay entitled 'The Wibelungen: World History as Told in Saga' Wagner examines the legend of the Ring. He acknowledges that the Nibelungen Hoard, the Ring treasure was transformed into the quest for the Grail. At the time of writing this essay he was in the process of unravelling the complex evidence he had amassed in his preliminary studies for the Ring. Writing to Mathilde Wessendonck in 1859 he noted that the Grail had been previously not a Cup but a stone which as he said 'could be traced back to the earliest sources, namely the Arabic texts of the Spanish Moors.'[68] He went on, 'However, the legends of its miraculous powers were soon interpreted by the christians after their OWN fashion.' In the 1849 'Die Wibelungen' he had perceived the whole mythic pattern. The Grail had been the Nibelungen Hoard which in turn traced back to the very source of the human story when it transformed to its primal reality a simple Black Stone, significant not for itself but for what it represented – the source of human religion in its original pure form.

> 'The quest of the Grail henceforth replaces the struggle for the Nibelungen Hoard; and, as the occidental world, unsatisfied spiritually, reached out past Rome and Pope to find its source of healing in the tomb of the Redeemer at Jerusalem, as, unsatisfied even there, it cast its yearning gaze, half spiritual, half physical, still further towards the East to find the primal shrine of mankind, so the Grail was said to have been withdrawn from our cynical West to the pure chaste unattainable birthplace of all nations.'[69]

And so, the Grail was nothing other than the Black Stone of the Ka'aba, the central shrine of the world's last religion, purified judaeo-christianity,

Islam. Makkah is named in the Qur'an as the Mother of Cities, and thus the 'birthplace of all nations' and the Ka'aba is named the 'primal shrine of all mankind'. Embedded in one corner of the Ka'aba stands the Black Stone which every muslim raises his lips to and kisses when he arrives dusty and exhausted as a pilgrim, kisses as if quenching his thirst. This is the extraordinary tale that Wagner has, partly despite himself, and partly aware, chosen to tell the world in his farewell revolutionary message. Both the Bey of Tunis and Abdalhamid II, Caliph of Islam, contributed to the foundation of Bayreuth, they had not yet heard Parsifal, but their hearts drew them to this most spiritual of men among men in an age of darkness. When Parsifal ends in its vast serenity, 'One of the most beautiful edifices in sound ever raised to the glory of music' as Debussy described it, a white dove descends and hovers over Parsifal – symbol of peace which in Arabic bears the same root 'S-L-M' as pure religion itself, Islam.

NOTES

1   Friedrich Nietzsche in: Kritische Studienausgabe
    (KSA), München 1967-77, Bd. 1, S. 891.
2   Wagners Brief an Minna Wagner vom 14. Mai 1849 in:
    Sämtliche Briefe, Leipzig 1970, Bd. II, S. 654.
3   Wagners Brief an Th. Uhlig vom 27. Dezember 1849
    in: Sämtliche Briefe, Leipzig 1975, Bd. III, S. 196.
4   Richard Wagner: Die Kunst und die Revolution. In:
    Gesammelte Schriften und Dichtungen, 2. Aufl.,
    Bd. 3, S. 2.
5   Richard Wagner: Oper und Drama. In: Gesammelte
    Schriften und Dichtungen, 2. Aufl., Bd. 4, S. 91.
6   a.a.O., S. 98.
7   Brief an Th. Uhlig vom 12.11.1851 in: Sämtliche
    Briefe, Leipzig 1969, Bd. IV, S. 176.
8   R. Wagner: Eine Mitteilung an meine Freunde. In:
    Gesammelte Schriften und Dichtungen, 2. Aufl., Bd.
    4, S. 279.
9   a.a.O., S. 266.
10 a.a.O., S.301 f.
11 Brief Wagners an Franz Liszt vom 30. Januar 1852.
12 Nietzsche: Der Wille zur Macht (602).
13 R. Wagner: Zukunftsmusik. In: Gesammelte Schriften
    und Dichtungen, Bd.7, S. 122f.
14 M. Heidegger: Nietzsche 1, 5. Aufl. 1989, S. 244.
15 a.a.O., S. 246.
16 a.a.O., S. 248.
17 a.a.O., S. 249.

18 Nietzsche KSA 13, 17 [3].
19 Goethe: Faust II, 3, Innerer Burghof. In: Hamburger
    Ausgabe, München 1982, Band II, S. 287.
20 Heidegger: Nietzsche I, S. 163 f.
21 a.a.O., S. 90.
22 Nietzsche: Der Wille zur Macht (853,11).
    In: KSA 13,17 [3].
23 Nietzsche: Menschliches, Allzumenschliches II,
    Vorrede 3.
24 a.a.O., Ende.
25 Brief Nietzsches an Franz Overbeck vom 22.2.1883.
26 Brief Nietzsches an Peter Gast vom 21.1.1887.
27 Nietzsche: Der Fall Wagner. 8.
28 Brief von Richard Strauß an Hugo von Hofmannstal
    vom 21.11.1928.
29 R. Wagner: Oper und Drama II,VI. In: Gesammelte
    Schriften und Dichtungen, 2. Aufl., Bd. 4, S. 97.
30 a.a.O., II, IV, Bd. 4, S.72.
31 a.a.O., I, VII, Bd. 3, S. 311.
32 a.a.O., S. 314.
33 a.a.O., I, V, Bd. 3, S. 276 f.
34 a.a.O., S. 279.
35 Brief Wagners an M. Wesendonck vom 29.10.1859. In:
    R. Wagner, Briefe, München 1983, S. 4.05.
36 Wagner: Was nützt uns diese Erkenntnis? In:
    Gesammelte Schriften und Dichtungen. 2. Aufl.,
    Bd. 10, S. 263.
37 Brief Wagners an Röckel vom 25./26. Januar 1854. In:
    Sämtliche Briefe, Leipzig 1986, Bd. VI, S. 69.
38 Brief Wagners an Julie Ritter vom 6. Mai 1857.
39 Brief Wagners an König Ludwig II. von Bayern vom
    23./24. Februar 1869.
40 Brief Wagners an Röckel vom 25./26. Januar 1854. In:
    Sämtliche Briefe, Leipzig 1986, Bd. VI, S. 67.

41   a.a.O., S. 60ff.
42   a.a.O., S. 69ff.
43   Nietzsche: KSA 13, 14 [123].
44   Rede Wagners vor dem Vaterlandsverein, Dresden, 15. Juni 1848.
45   R. Wagner: Oper und Drama II, IV. In: Gesammelte Schriften und Dichtungen, 2. Aufl., Bd. 4, S. 73.
46   Nietzsche in: KSA 1, 485.
47   Heidegger: Nietzsche II, 40.
48   Nietzsche: Also sprach Zarathustra II. Von der Erlösung.
49   Heidegger: Nietzsche II, 39.
50   a.a.O., S. 264.
51   Rede Wagners vor dem Vaterlandsverein, Dresden, 15. Juni 1848.
52   Nietzsche: Also sprach Zarathustra III. Der Genesende. 1.
53   Heidegger: Nietzsche II, 283.
54   a.a.O., S. 286.
55   a.a.O., I, S.312.
56   Heidegger: Wer ist Nietzsches Zarathustra? In: Vorträge und Aufsätze. 6. Auflage 1990, S. 121.
57   Heidegger: Nietzsche II, S. 304.
58   Heidegger: Wer ist Nietzsches Zarathustra? In: Vorträge und Aufsätze. 6. Auflage 1990, S. 102f.
59   a.a.O., S. 114.
60   Wagners Brief an Th. Uhlig vom 27. Dezember 1849.
61   Wagners Brief an Liszt vom September 1860.
62   Wagner: Über deutsches Musikwesen. In: Gesammelte Schriften und Dichtungen, 2. Aufl., Bd. 1, S. 160.
63   Brief an Herrn von Stein vom 31. Januar 1883.
64   Brief Wagners an Hans von Wolzogen vom 17.1.1880. In: R. Wagner, Briefe 1830-1883, Berlin 1986, S. 428.
65   a.a.O., S. 428 f.

66   Rede Wagners vor dem Vaterlandsverein, Dresden,
      15. Juni 1848.
67   Wagners Brief an Th. Uhlig vom 14.10.1852. In:
      Sämtliche Briefe, Leipzig 1993, Bd. V, S. 80.
68   Wagners Brief an M. Wesendonck vom 29./30. Mai
      1859. In: R. Wagner, Briefe, München 1983, S. 396.
69   Die Wibelungen. In: R. Wagner, Gesammelte Schriften
      und Dichtungen, 2. Aufl., Bd. 2, S. 151 f.

A NOTE ON THE TYPE

This book was set in Adobe Garamond. Designed for
the Adobe Corporation by Robert Slimbach, the fonts
are based on types first cut by Claude Garamond
(c. 1480–1561). Garamond was a pupil of Geoffroy
Tory and is believed to have followed the Venetian
models, although he introduced a number of
important differences, and it is to him that we owe the
letter we now know as "old style". He gave his letters
a certain elegance and feeling of movement that won
their creator an immediate reputation and the
patronage of Francis I of France.